More than Happy

The Wisdom of Amish Parenting

Serena B. Miller

with Paul Stutzman

HOWARD BOOKS
AN IMPRINT OF SIMON & SCHUSTER, INC.

New York   Nashville   London   Toronto   Sydney   New Delhi

Howard Books
An Imprint of Simon & Schuster, Inc.
1230 Avenue of the Americas
New York, NY 10020

Some names and identifying characteristics have been changed.

First Howard Books trade paperback edition May 2016

HOWARD and colophon are trademarks of Simon & Schuster, Inc.

For information about special discounts for bulk purchases, please contact Simon & Schuster Special Sales at 1-866-506-1949 or business@simonandschuster.com.

The Simon & Schuster Speakers Bureau can bring authors to your live event. For more information or to book an event, contact the Simon & Schuster Speakers Bureau at 1-866-248-3049 or visit our website at www.simonspeakers.com.

Interior design by Jill Putorti

Manufactured in the United States of America

10 9 8 7 6 5 4 3 2 1

Library of Congress Cataloging-in-Publication Data is available.

ISBN 978-1-4767-5340-9
ISBN 978-1-5011-4360-1 (pbk)
ISBN 978-1-4767-5341-6 (ebook)

With thanks to Joyanne and Clay Ham—who opened the door
and
my Amish friends for their patience, wisdom, and hospitality

Contents

Introduction

"Amish parenting isn't a method. It is a way of life."
—PAUL STUTZMAN

I barely noticed the white van sitting at the gas pumps beside me. It was late. I was tired. It was winter and the roads were slick. My home in southern Ohio was still fifteen miles away and I was in a hurry to get there.

The gas pumps were old and did not take credit cards. I was annoyed that I had to enter the small convenience store to pay. I was also worried about a friend in the hospital I had been visiting earlier. My fatigue and concerns totally absorbed me.

As I entered, I was surprised to see an Amish mother standing there with a baby in her arms. Two small boys and their little sister were beside her. The mother wore a black dress that came down to her ankles, a black bonnet, black coat, black shoes, black dress, black stockings. She glanced up as I came through the door, and gave me a sweet smile before turning her attention back to her three children, who were giving serious consideration to the candy rack.

I poured myself some coffee while the children quietly conferred on their choice of candy. The baby, wide awake, contentedly peered out from her mother's arms.

Decision made, the oldest one—a little boy about eight years old—reached for three Tootsie Pops of various flavors. He handed the candy to his mother and then kept a watchful eye on his little brother and sister while the mother produced a black purse and paid the cashier.

A moment later, when she handed her children their treats, I heard each one politely say something that sounded like they were thanking her in a foreign language. The family went outside, the man driving the van helped them into the vehicle, and they drove off into the night as the cashier and I watched in silence.

Once they were out of sight, the young cashier shook her head in wonder. "I see all kinds of people in here, but the Amish children amaze me. They are so well behaved and polite. Even the babies seem more content than our kids. I wish I knew how their parents do it. I try to be a good mother, but my two kids act like wild animals compared to the Amish children I see in here."

"What were they doing here?" I asked. "And why a van? I thought those people rode around in buggies."

"The driver said he'd been hired to bring them back from a funeral." She shrugged. "I guess maybe they're allowed to ride in vans if there is a death in the family."

As I drove away, I kept thinking about that family and how odd it had felt to see children who were so polite and well behaved. Even though I could not understand a word they said, it was obvious there had been no quarreling between them as they discussed which candy to choose, and it had seemed as natural as breathing to them to murmur their gratitude when their mother handed them their candy.

The whole scenario brought back one night several years earlier, when we were living in Detroit and I had helped a nonprofit group sell souvenirs at a Detroit Lions football game. We had pennants and T-shirts and all sorts of knickknacks with logos on them. It was an important game and dozens of parents and their children came through the line. At times they came so fast that the faces and voices became a blur as I tried to keep up with the demand.

Then something happened that made me stop and stare. A boy, about twelve years old, watched as his father bought him a T-shirt, and then he said, "Thank you, Dad. I really appreciate you getting this for me." It was such a simple thing to say, except that this was the first child in a long night of sales who had taken the time to say thank you. Most of the children seemed to take the gifts for granted or were unhappy that they weren't getting more stuff. I had tuned out the whining and occasional tantrum, but was stopped cold by that one heartfelt thank you, and I have never forgotten it.

That's how it felt inside the convenience store that winter night. I felt sad that the clerk and I, both of us mothers, would be so stunned by what should have been normal behavior.

It also struck me that this was the first time I had ever glimpsed an Amish person up close. It felt like I had witnessed an alien culture. Even the Amish woman's sweet smile of welcome as I came through the door was different from the usual get-in-get-out-don't-make-eye-contact attitude that most people adopt when making a purchase in a convenience store.

I found myself wishing I could have spent time with that Amish mother. Talked with her. Found out more about her life. She had a quiet presence that made me wish we could be friends.

I soon discovered that this would not be the last time I would come face-to-face with the Amish. A local farmer informed me that they were actually starting to move to southern Ohio in fairly large numbers. I asked why. Because of the abandoned farms and cheap land, he told me. He was pleased. The Amish are known for helping stabilize an agricultural area. They are true farmers, he said.

I was delighted when a few months later an Amish produce stand appeared in a parking lot outside an auto repair shop in Muletown, Ohio—only ten minutes from my home. I was grateful for the mounds of locally grown produce the Amish farmer brought, but I was absolutely fascinated by the fact that the father usually brought one or two children with him to spend the day, even though they were sometimes too young to be of any real help. Yet again, I noticed the unusually contented behavior of the Amish children. The little ones were amazingly well behaved as they tried to help their father in whatever small ways they could.

Within weeks, I saw another Amish business going up. A bakery was built beside a back road that was so out of the way I pitied the family who was going to all that trouble and expense when I knew their little business would fail. It simply had to. It was in the middle of nowhere. There were no other businesses for miles around, or even any towns nearby from which to draw customers.

What I did not know was that a handful of Amish women would soon begin turning out the biggest, fluffiest, most delicious doughnuts any of us had ever tasted. They even set up a front porch where customers were welcome to sit and rock and munch on doughnuts and other baked goods. The porch had been thoughtfully furnished with solid, locally made Amish rocking chairs and outdoor furniture . . . complete with price tags.

I soon discovered that, far from being a failure, the out-of-the-way bakery was quickly becoming so successful that it was wise to call ahead and reserve a box of doughnuts before driving all the way out there. Even in the middle of nowhere, that bakery sold out *fast*.

A few miles from the bakery, a young Amish couple started a small home business. They did nothing in the way of advertisement except put a handmade sign at the end of their driveway. The sign said that they would sew or upholster anything. The building from which they worked was not large. There was a workshop on the bottom, and the family, with their stair-step children, lived above.

People began arriving with shabby furniture. Then they began telling others about the excellent workmanship and fair prices. Soon, the upholsterer and his wife were up to their ears with work. Within two years they moved their young family from the top of the upholstery shop to a large, new house they had built.

All this productivity caused me to grow more and more curious about the Amish culture. Who were these people who created flourishing home businesses where none had existed and then bravely (foolishly?) used horses and buggies as conveyances on our backcountry roads? Who were these people who took long-abandoned farms and turned them into agricultural showpieces using only horse-drawn power?

I saw them shopping at Walmart, dressed as though they had stepped out of the 1800s, and was surprised to see them buying items that did not fit at all with my idea of who the Amish were supposed to be. Who knew that an Amish teenage boy could spend so long pondering the various types of hair products, or that an Amish woman would allow herself to longingly finger a piece of a brightly flowered fabric?

Like most "Englisch" (the name by which the Amish refer to anyone who is not part of their culture), I watched them, privately wondering what it was that drove them to dress and live so differently. Why did they sacrifice so much convenience in the name of their religion? I, too, was seriously committed to my Christian faith, but I saw nothing in the Bible that commanded me to give up electricity and cars. Did this group of people actually believe it was necessary to forgo such things as electric lights in order to assure their place in heaven? Most puzzling of all, why were the Amish children I saw so well-behaved and obedient? Was that a good thing? Or did it hint at dark threats and violence at home?

One morning, as I started to drive out of Walmart's parking lot, I found myself beside a young Amish man in a horse and buggy who was preparing to turn left as I prepared to turn right. As we waited for the light to change, I glanced into his buggy and was astonished to see a sparkly Jeff Gordon sticker attached to the inside front of the buggy where the dash of a car would be. Beside the sticker was another one that said NASCAR. Beneath both words were stick-on letters spelling out GIT ER DONE.

Before I could react, the light changed, the sober-looking Amish man clucked his tongue at his horse, and although they trotted off down the road at about ten miles per hour, I had a suspicion that in his heart the young man was imagining himself behind the wheel of a race car. Either that or he had an excellent sense of humor. Neither of which fit my preconceived ideas of the Amish culture.

A few months earlier, I had signed on with a literary agent who was trying hard to interest a publisher in my first two suspense novels. She wasn't having much luck and I was growing discouraged. Then one day she called and my fledgling writing career took a sudden and unexpected turn.

"Your last name is Miller and you live in Ohio," she said. I didn't realize it at the time, but Miller is a very common Amish name, and Ohio has one of the largest concentrations of Amish in the world. "Do you happen to know any Amish people?"

Her question was puzzling. She was entirely too busy to chat on the phone with her authors just for the fun of it. When she called, it was always related to business.

"At the moment, there are a couple of Amish men putting in a storage barn behind my house," I answered. "But I don't really know them. Why?"

"I have an editor who is looking for a romance novel set in Ohio Amish country. She's willing to look at a proposal if you're interested."

My mind whirled. I admired what I had seen of the Amish culture, but not once had it occurred to me to write a book about them. On the other hand, getting hired by a royalty-paying book publisher was not easy. I knew that this was an opportunity I could not pass up.

"Tell me what to do," I said.

A month later, I found myself driving three hours north to Sugarcreek, Ohio, a village located in Tuscarawas County, hoping to write what would become my first published book.

Although some Amish families had moved to our area in southern Ohio, they were still very much in the minority. When I entered true "Amish Country" (the three counties that make up the largest settlement of Amish in the world), I felt like I had stepped back in time.

The fall weather was perfect. Amish men were in the fields harvesting their crops with old-fashioned farming equipment. Farm wagons were hitched to highly trained workhorses while men and boys expertly guided as many as six abreast with leather reins. Cows grazed in vibrantly green rolling fields. A milk tanker wound its way along a narrow country road, taking its rich load to one of the many award-winning local cheese factories.

Fields were dotted with the type of teepee-like corn shocks that I had seen only in idyllic rural paintings. Roadside stands sold the final gleanings of summer produce. Amish women in dresses and bonnets worked in flower gardens and teenage girls in pastel dresses cleared fencerows with—to my surprise—gasoline-powered lawn trimmers.

Pink-cheeked, barefoot Amish children played outdoors at nearly every farm I passed. A gaggle of Amish women sat on a front porch, talking and laughing while stringing green beans. The place was so picturesque it seemed like there should have been music just naturally playing in the background.

I had made arrangements to stay at the Oak Haven Bed and Breakfast for no other reason than that it was in the heart of Amish country and affordable. When I arrived, I discovered that Oak Haven's proprietors, Joyanne and Clay Ham, were transplants from Texas who had fallen in love with the area while passing through and had purchased and restored an old farmhouse, planning to rent out rooms to tourists.

Their B&B was not yet generating enough income for them to live on entirely, and so, in addition to taking in paying guests, they took on the job of becoming professional "Yoder Toters," an Amish tongue-in-cheek term for Englisch drivers who make their living by transporting Amish to doctor visits, shopping trips, weddings, funerals, and anywhere else they need to go.

Most people know that the Old Order Amish believe in owning only horse-drawn vehicles. Possessing an automobile is forbidden and an Old Order Amish person would be asked to leave the church if he or she purchased one. However, riding in someone else's car is allowed. Therefore, when their destination is farther than the approximately ten miles they believe a horse pulling a buggy should travel, they hire a multipassenger van, much like someone in the city might hire a taxi.

Learning of this, Joyanne and Clay purchased two vans and began generating a second income by taking their Amish neighbors wherever they needed to go. These road trips eventually led to close friendships between the Hams and their Amish passengers, friendships that Joyanne says changed her life.

"They accepted me for who I was," Joyanne told me. "They loved me in spite of my flaws. I have learned so much from them. Moving here has been one of the greatest blessings of my life."

The first evening I spent with Joyanne and Clay, we sat up late discussing some of the things they had learned about their Amish friends' culture. One comment Joyanne made stayed with me long after I went to bed.

"I am convinced that the Amish have the happiest children in the world."

I flashed back to the night I'd watched the Amish mother and her children in the gas station convenience store.

"Why do you think that is?" I asked.

"I'll show you tomorrow," she promised. "Clay and I are invited to one of our Amish friends' home for dinner. I'll call and see if it's okay to bring you along."

The next evening we had supper with Naomi and Luke, an Old Order Amish couple who live on a nearby farm. They had seven children still at home. It was warm for September and the Amish don't have air-conditioning, so Naomi had chosen to set her dinner outdoors on a makeshift table. The older children's friends had dropped by for a friendly volleyball game. The huge kettle of vegetable beef soup their mother had made for dinner fed quite a crowd.

It was an otherworldly experience for me, watching barefoot girls in old-fashioned long dresses hit the volleyball over the net while handsome teenage boys scrambled to hit it back to them.

Early in the game, I saw one of the older teenagers notice a little boy cousin, about ten years old, quietly watching the bigger kids play. The older boy stopped the game long enough to invite the younger child to join them—which the little boy was happy to do. None of the teenagers complained about the addition, even though the child was not old enough to be as good a player as the rest of them. It was obvious that winning the game was a whole lot less important to any of them than making sure the younger boy felt included.

From time to time, as the adults visited, the telephone in the phone shanty at the end of the driveway would ring. It was early Friday night and other teenagers from other farms were checking in to make plans. I found it amusing when, like so many other parents of teenage children, the father would yell, "Would one of you children get that?" before going back to his conversation with Clay and my husband.

It was such a pretty sight. The girls in their dresses of various shades of pink, rose, and blue. The boys in short-sleeved white or blue shirts and dark pants. The girls, for the most part, wore white kerchiefs over their hair, which they had braided and pinned up. The boys, most of whom who were older than sixteen and therefore into what some people call their *rumspringa* (running around) period, were allowed Englisch-style haircuts. The little boy cousin still had his hair chopped off below his ears like his father and the other Amish men.

All this activity was played out against a backdrop of rolling fields and faraway barns. The family's solid, large house sat on a hill that dropped away to a gorgeous view of the setting sun. Flowers decorated the porch and yard. A girl about eight years old sat on the grass near the father's lawn chair, cuddling a kitten. The youngest, a little girl about four years old, sat at her mother's feet, contentedly playing with a pile of pebbles. A Lassie-type dog was curled up asleep beside her. An older daughter, about twelve, was in a pasture next to the yard, working at training a horse.

"That's Anna," her mother said fondly. "She's so good with horses."

It felt like I had somehow managed to stumble accidentally onto the set of *Little House on the Prairie*, except that this was real, and what I was seeing was simply part of this family's day-to-day life.

The child who impressed me the most was the littlest daughter. I had never been around a child that age who could be so content for so long simply making designs on the ground with pebbles. She did not interrupt our conversation, although she glanced up from her play every now and then when there was laughter, and she would smile, as though enjoying the fact that her mother and father and their guests were having a good time.

With the exception of the father's occasional exasperation over the phone ringing in the family's phone shanty, there was not the slightest hint of parental discipline. Neither the mother nor the father chastised any of the children. Instead, they seemed to take their children's calm behavior for granted, and I discovered later in our relationship that they could afford to do so because these children were not just obedient and content . . . they were remarkably happy.

There was no whining, no constant interruptions, no tattling. This behavior was extraordinarily different from many of my experiences with Englisch children—including my own three sons.

When my sons were small, it seemed impossible to have a conversation without being interrupted every few seconds. Especially if I was talking with a friend who also had young children. I had recently commiserated with two young mothers who were trying to set up a time to get together when one of them joked that since they could talk for only ninety-second bursts without interruption, it would be prudent if they prepared their stories ahead of time accordingly.

Later, after that first dinner with the Amish, Joyanne and I decided that if it were possible for us to invent a pill that would bring such peace and contentment to a home as what we'd just witnessed, we would be rich within a week.

The novel I wrote about Sugarcreek was published the next year and was well received. I grew so interested in the culture that I wrote and researched several more Amish novels.

The Amish families I met while researching those novels amazed me with their heartfelt hospitality. As I visited with, ate with, and worked with various Amish families, I continued to be impressed with their industriousness and with their children. What were they doing right? What were we missing out on? As a mother and grandmother, I studied these families, hoping to discover their secrets for raising contented children.

Even though my own children are grown, for the past twenty years, my husband has ministered to a church consisting of around three hundred people. At present, about a third of the congregation are children under the age of twelve.

I am impressed with the dedication of our young parents. They are so very earnest and they try so hard and yet I see the fatigue and stress in their faces. I hear their frustrations in trying to discipline their children. I hear them express disappointment in themselves for resorting to using television and electronic devices to keep their children occupied. I watch quarrels among siblings and disrespect of one another as the children interact. I watch the elderly of our congregation clutch at pews for stability as children careen past them, ignoring their parents' admonishments not to run in the church building.

As a parent, I can relate. I've often said that I think my sons turned out okay in spite of me, because it isn't as though I knew what I was doing. My husband and I just stumbled through the best we could.

Yet, as a grandmother and minister's wife, I am sometimes asked advice on raising children. I never know what to say. If I'm completely honest, my method of child rearing could be summed up in seven words: "Keep them alive and pray a lot."

But, as I spent more time with Amish children, I began to wonder if the study of the Amish culture could give me any helpful clues about parenting, clues that could also be used in non-Amish homes. What could we learn from this culture that seemed so different from ours, but seemed to be getting so many things right?

I began to make a serious study of what, exactly, Amish parents were doing differently. I talked with Amish new mothers and great-grandmothers, fathers, grandfathers, and Amish ministers. Why were their children so respectful? Why did they eat everything on their plates at mealtimes? Why did the Amish mothers I met—with no help from electric labor-saving appliances—seem so much less stressed than the non-Amish mothers I knew?

This book is an attempt to capture the lessons about parenting that I've gleaned from Amish parents over a period of several years. I hope to share what I've learned, though I make no claims to being an expert. My viewpoint will always be that of an outsider, an observer, looking in.

I did not want this book to be based entirely upon my own flawed observations, so I asked Paul Stutzman, a Mennonite writer who was born to Old Order Amish parents, to help provide insight into what an Amish childhood truly entails.

Paul's background is a mixture of Amish and Mennonite cultures. His parents left the Amish church while he was still small and they joined a conservative Mennonite church. Their lives changed little, he says, with the exception of owning a car. They still wore plain dress, spoke in Pennsylvania Dutch, and devoted themselves to living lives that honored God. He spent weeks at a time in the summer visiting his Amish grandmother's farm.

Paul and I raised our children under very different circumstances. Paul and his wife provided a safe, rural environment for their three children, surrounded by the comforting presence of their extended Amish and Mennonite families. They lived within a few miles of where he grew up, in the lovely Holmes County, Ohio, area.

My husband and I, on the other hand, primarily raised our three sons in the Detroit, Michigan, area, with both of our extended families living several hundred miles away. We worried daily about drive-by shootings, were supervigilant about possible kidnappings, and pondered what to do about the thriving marijuana patch in one next-door neighbor's backyard.

Neither Paul nor I believe that today's parents must disconnect from electricity, drive around with horse and buggies, and live on a working farm in order to build healthy, happy, supportive families. Nor do we believe that Amish homes are without problems. The Amish would be the first to point out that they are an imperfect people.

We believe, however, that there is much wisdom to be gleaned from the Amish that can be successfully applied to parenting within non-Amish homes. Though it is impossible to talk about the Amish without their strong faith entering into the discussion, and though my own perspective as someone who has served in ministry for decades will inevitably come through, this book is not meant only for those interested in faith-based parenting principles. I believe the advice the Amish community shared with me is much broader, and much more applicable to our society at large, than that. I hope those who read this book will find something useful regardless of their religious backgrounds.

The Amish are a humble people. *Hochmut* (haughtiness or pride) is considered a sin and they carefully avoid it. They would never put themselves forward as experts in child rearing. Pride is so despised that even within the haven of their own worship services, a minister will almost always humbly invite others to correct him.

When I asked Amish people for advice about child rearing, I could tell that it went against their nature to act as though they thought they had any wisdom at all to give. However, helping one's neighbor is also deeply woven into the fabric of their lives. For the sake of the Englisch children, they reluctantly began to give opinions and answers to my questions. I soon discovered that they had more to say than even I had realized.

In many ways this book is a gift from their homes to yours. I pray that it will somehow prove to be helpful.

· I ·

Family

Family

"Our babies are constantly in the middle of everything."
—AMISH MOTHER

As I set out to try to understand what makes Amish children, in the words of my friend Joyanne, "the happiest kids on earth," the natural place to start seemed to be to gather a group of Amish women and ask them questions about their parenting techniques. I decided to host a luncheon and invite all the Old Order Amish women I'd gotten to know from my research trips to the area. Their ages spread across four generations. The youngest was a new mother in her early twenties with a three-week-old baby in her arms. The oldest was a great-grandmother who had more than seventy grandchildren living in the immediate area. They were aware that they were going to be interrogated about Amish parenting at this luncheon and they were good-humored about it.

I'd read countless parenting books as I had raised my children, and each seemed to promise some miracle technique or philosophy that would lead to happier, healthier children. My daughter-in-law was now pregnant with her first child, and we'd discussed many of the issues in the newest parenting books she was reading. She'd brought up topics like feeding on demand versus scheduling, breast or bottle, buying baby food versus making your own, vaccinating or not, Ferberizing versus the family bed—all hot-button topics in the mainstream parenting advice market.

I was prepared with a list of questions about topics that seem to incite angst and emotional reactions in the Englisch mothers I knew. I was sure that, with the results I'd seen, these women must have strong opinions and an overarching philosophy that guided their parenting decisions.

"I want to find out why Amish children are so content," I said as we sat down to a picnic-type meal of chicken, baked beans, and potato salad. I glanced at my list of questions. "Let's start with infants. Do you feed on demand, or do you stick to a rigid schedule?"

This was a question my daughter-in-law had asked me especially to find out. As a soon-to-be new mother, she was trying so hard to figure out how to do everything right. Whether or not to breast-feed on demand, or put a baby on a schedule, and if so, *when* to put a baby on a feeding schedule were big topics of conversation with her and many of the other new mothers at our church.

"I think our babies are usually fed on demand," the young Amish mother said tentatively, though she looked a bit confused.

"Mine are, but I'm having a hard time nursing Jonas right now. It's like something bothers him," said another.

"Mine were all fed on demand," Barbara, a mother of eight, volunteered. "But I noticed that they demanded it a lot more when I had not eaten well. What a mother eats has a real effect on her nursing baby. If she doesn't eat nourishing food, the baby doesn't get the nutrition it needs and naturally nurses more. I've noticed it's the same way with cows and their calves. If a cow has poor nutrition, the calf can't seem to nurse enough. My babies were always more easily satisfied when I paid attention to getting the right foods in me."

I scribbled notes. I knew that this particular woman once helped her husband run a dairy farm while nursing eight babies. What she said about babies and calves was probably well worth listening to. I suspected a number of the Englisch moms I knew would have a hard time being compared to a dairy cow, but it seemed to be a natural reference for the Amish mothers. Several nodded in agreement.

"What about baby food? Do you buy commercial or make your own?" I asked.

The mothers looked at one another as if they were not sure they understood the question.

A young mother finally answered. "A lot of women buy some baby food in jars, but also mash some food at the table. I did that for my daughter, Miriam, but intend to make my own for Jonas and freeze it in ice cube trays."

"What about sleep?" I asked. "Do Amish babies sleep in a separate room or with the mother and father?"

"Right now we have Miriam's and Jonas's beds in our room," the woman continued. "It makes it easier for me to get stuff for them. And it makes it easy to nurse Jonas at night. I also have a rocker in our room."

"Is that usual in Amish families?" I asked. "Children sleeping in the same room with the parents?"

Again there was a pause, as if they were trying to understand what I was getting at.

"I don't know what other families do," one said tentatively. "But I remember sleeping in my parents' bed sometimes if there was a thunderstorm. It would have been so scary if they had sent me back to my room, but they were always understanding about it. I remember thinking I would be safe from anything if I could just be with them."

Her mother smiled. "You were never a bother. We didn't want you to be frightened."

This reminded me of another question my daughter-in-law wanted me to ask.

"How do any of you feel about allowing a child to cry it out?"

A few of the women looked at each other, and I saw one of them give a little shrug.

"What do you mean?" The grandmother, who was sitting beside me turned to look directly at me, and I saw a worried expression on her face. "Cry it out?"

"I'm talking about putting a child to bed in a separate room and letting them cry themselves to sleep."

"Never!" The great-grandmother shook her head emphatically, then hugged herself and gave a little shiver. "I cannot bear to even think of it."

"There are some experts who really advocate this method of training a child to go to sleep on their own," I explained.

"We're not real comfortable with that," Barbara said uneasily. There was a pause, and then someone elaborated. "We rarely put our babies in a separate room even for their naps. We prefer for them to be with us or with older brothers and sisters."

I decided to leave that subject. "What about vaccinating?"

Yet again, they looked at each other as though trying to puzzle out what I was asking.

"Serena, we thought you wanted to know what makes Amish children so content," one of them finally said.

"I do. That's what I'm trying to figure out," I said.

There was another pause, and then Barbara nodded toward the youngest mother in our group, who was holding her new baby over her shoulder. "Do you see that?"

I nodded.

"Our children are used to being around lots of family from long before they are born. A young mother is seldom left on her own. She always has help. We spend so much time with our families that I think it helps give our children a feeling of security. Babies are nearly always being held by someone, and they are constantly in the middle of everything."

Slowly, it began to dawn on me what she was getting at. Amish families are large, and extended families often live in close proximity. Family members are constantly in and out of each other's homes. There would be no place to be alone, even if you wanted to be. From the time they are infants, children live in a society where they are surrounded by people who care about them, a culture that is intentionally built around the importance of family and community.

An infant doesn't understand the implications of that, but he does feel the security of having all his needs met, of knowing that there are always people around who care. What Barbara was saying is that one of the reasons Amish children are so content is because they are born into a community structured to make the family central, and this allows children to feel secure.

As I probed further into Amish parenting, I quickly realized that Amish parenting is not a "method"; it is the culmination of many beliefs deeply held by the entire community. One of the most important of those beliefs is that the family will be at the center of just about everything Amish people do. Even more than I had originally thought. Every decision, every choice, is made with the good of the family in mind, and the entire Amish culture is built around preserving and protecting the family unit. After my realization at the luncheon, it seemed an appropriate place to start digging a bit more deeply into the wisdom of Amish parenting.

Marriage in a Horse-and-Buggy Society

"You're going to an Amish wedding? Oh, you will eat so well!"
—MENNONITE BOOKSTORE OWNER

The family unit is so important in Amish culture that its central role is emphasized to their children in both word and deed from the time the child is born. Long before an Amish couple becomes a family, they have been steeped in the teaching that the family unit is to be honored and protected one's entire life. I discovered the depth of this teaching when I accidentally invited myself to an Amish wedding.

I was visiting my Old Order Amish friend Mary and her family one evening. Mary has become one of my closest friends. I trust her, admire her, and frequently wish I were more like her. Mary is, incidentally, quite beautiful. I say "incidentally" because a person's outward beauty is not emphasized in the Amish culture. Her resemblance to Ingrid Bergman is of no interest to her, especially since she's never heard of Ingrid Bergman.

Mary covers her pretty blond hair with a white prayer *kapp*. In the summer she wears loose, pastel dresses while doing household chores. In the fall, she supplements her wardrobe with a tan work sweater and black rubber boots before heading out to the barn to milk her cow and feed her chickens and barn cats. In the winter, she adds a heavy black coat and a head scarf. Fashion is not something she worries about as long as she's in obedience to the Ordnung, the rules of unity and order that her church agrees to observe each year.

I'm a little envious of the ease of their clothing because I've never quite known how to dress myself. It seems as if other women inherited a basic clothing instinct that I'm missing. For an Amish woman, however, the style never changes.

This has many benefits. Mary can whip up a simple dress for herself in an afternoon on her treadle sewing machine, and so can each of her older daughters. In addition to that, their dresses are inexpensive. They cost no more than a length of plain fabric and some thread. There are no buttons or zippers to worry about. Makeup and jewelry are not part of their ensemble.

Being clean, modest, obedient to God, and a good wife and mother are Mary's highest priorities. She is one of the most contented and peaceful women I've ever known. She is, moreover, a stunner, and so are her seven children, which include five daughters, the eldest twenty-one and the youngest five. Her two sons are nearly grown, unmarried, live at home, and contribute heavily to the family finances with their incomes as carpenters.

I've noticed that she and her husband talk to each other and about each other with respect. I notice that he listens carefully to her when she speaks to him, and even with company in the house (me), she takes the time to question him about his day and carefully listens to his answer when he comes home from his work at the furniture shop. The children respect this time between their mother and father and do not interrupt.

This couple does not use the word *love* overmuch in their household. It is not a word tossed about cheaply. Instead, from what I can see, love simply shines through in their actions, showering their children and all who come beneath their roof with a sense of blessing and peace.

Mary sometimes affectionately refers to her sober, hardworking Amish husband as a "wildman." John smiles and agrees with her description of him. Yes, indeed, he is a wildman. He has big ideas and big dreams—all of which, I find, have to do with providing a more secure life for his family. In his mind, a more secure life does not necessarily mean a bigger house or deeper bank account. His greatest dream is to figure out a way to make his living entirely upon their hilly acreage. This is the ideal for Amish fathers, the life toward which most strive. The best life, in an Amish man's mind, is one in which he has meaningful work that puts him in close daily contact with his wife and children.

I enjoy staying with this couple and their family and they always make me feel welcome. The huge kitchen table easily seats all of us, with room to spare. There is much talking and laughing around that table. I have found that, in an Amish home, with no television or computers to distract, their guests and each other are the primary source of entertainment.

That evening, there were ten of us adults relaxing in folding chairs beneath the comforting shade of an ancient maple tree. I was grateful to John and Mary's extended family, who had also allowed me to enter their world and ask them questions. As a small thank-you, I was giving the women a break from cooking by ordering a towering stack of pizzas. I wanted to make sure everyone could eat their fill, and they had, including the children, who occasionally broke away from their play from time to time to run over and grab another piece of pizza or some of the cake that an aunt named Deborah had brought.

Susan, Mary's five-year-old daughter, ran up to her mother and rattled off a question.

"We have a guest," Mary gently reminded her.

The child glanced over her shoulder at me, gave me an apologetic grin, and then switched smoothly to English as she asked permission to have another piece of cake.

"Such a sweet tooth," Mary said fondly, and gave her permission.

Then the conversation returned to the topic at hand—the upcoming wedding of Levi and Deborah's eldest daughter.

"So, how many chickens do you think we'll need to butcher in order to feed everyone?" Levi asked as we relaxed and visited. Everyone was close kin to him, except me.

Because Levi was the father of the bride-to-be, the wedding was weighing heavily on his shoulders. This daughter was the first of his many chicks to leave the nest. Just like with Englisch weddings, there was a bittersweet quality to discussing the upcoming event. They liked the boy, but Levi and Deborah grieved the fact that their daughter was moving so far away.

Five miles.

"I know that doesn't seem like so much to you," Deborah had said to me earlier, "but with a horse and buggy, it is a lot to us."

"We'll need to feed around five hundred people before the day is over," the grandmother said.

No one ran for the calculator, because Levi's question about the number of chickens was rhetorical. They knew exactly how many chickens they would need and how many quarts of home canned green beans and how much celery and flowers and everything else that they would have to grow or gather or borrow. The Amish are experts at marrying off their children, and the chicken would be one of the greatest expenses. Fortunately, the father of the bride was a chicken farmer, which, under the circumstances, seemed a very good thing.

I was intrigued by this, and was very curious about what an Amish wedding would be like. I assumed it would be an informal affair along the lines of a barn raising, a sort of come-as-you-are function with piles of food laid out potluck-style on makeshift tables. I envisioned, after a brief ceremony, the couple riding off in a buggy decorated with flowers. I wanted to go, and I figured it wouldn't be too much of an imposition to ask if I could attend. I mean, what's one more person at a big church potluck. Right?

"I apologize for asking," I said, "but would it be rude if I came? I'd love to see a real Amish wedding."

There was a hesitation as they pondered my request. I attributed that hesitation to what my husband and I call the "Amish pause." These people are taught to take time to think before they speak, so it came as no surprise that my abrupt question required a few beats of quiet contemplation before answering.

My style of speech has frequently been described by my family as "shooting from the hip," so I find this pause of theirs fascinating. Try as I might, I can't seem to achieve it.

It is a full two months later before I realize that this particular hesitation had more to do with the fact that the father and mother of the bride were mentally shifting seats around in their heads and wondering where on earth they would put me. They had not counted on an Englisch woman suddenly inviting herself to the wedding, but they politely agreed that it would be fine if I wanted to come and I eagerly wrote down the date.

Sometimes it seems as though I have a great talent for making a *dumkopf* of myself around my Amish friends. I never mean any harm and they know that, which I suppose is why they have made a habit of forgiving my ignorance as I stumble through their lives. At the time, I had no idea how carefully planned out this wedding already was. To this day, I wonder who gave up their seat for me.

I was signing books at a local bookstore the next day when Deborah and her daughter Rebecca walked in.

"This is for you." Rebecca handed me a thick, high-quality envelope, which I opened. Inside was an elegant, professionally printed invitation to her wedding. This was the first I realized that the Amish purchase and mail out formal wedding invitations. I had assumed an Amish wedding would be a simple, word-of-mouth thing.

After they left, I showed the invitation to Eli, the bookstore owner. He was excited for me.

"An Amish wedding?" he said. "Oh, you are going to eat so well on that day!"

That evening, when I got home, I attached the wedding invitation to my refrigerator door. The next morning, I glanced at it again and did a double take. There was an obvious printing error. The invitation said that the wedding was to take place at 8:30 a.m. on a Thursday morning. I put on my reading glasses to make sure. Yes, that's what it said, 8:30 a.m.

As a minister's wife, I've been to a *lot* of weddings. I've sung for several of them and decorated for others. I've helped pin brides into borrowed wedding gowns, and eaten more wilted salads at receptions than I care to count. I've been to afternoon weddings, right-before-noon weddings, evening weddings, late-afternoon weddings, weddings in the woods, weddings on the beach, second weddings, fourth weddings, weddings to renew vows. But never, *ever*, had I seen a wedding take place at 8:30 a.m. on a Thursday morning.

I immediately phoned Joyanne and asked if they had made a mistake in the printing of the invitation. She laughed and said that this was the customary time for Amish weddings to take place. I asked why on earth they would begin that early in the morning. She gave me the same answer she had been given when she had asked. It is "tradition," she said.

She also told me that there would be about three hours of preaching before the actual ceremony took place around noon. "And everything will be conducted in German," she said.

Three hours of preaching? In a language I didn't understand? For a moment I wondered if it was too late to get out of going— but I was so curious about what it would be like to attend an Amish wedding, I figured a good night's sleep and a couple cups of coffee would get me through it.

The morning of the wedding, Joyanne and I arrived at the large, working farm and parked alongside dozens of black buggies in a field across the county road from the house. It was a gorgeous fall day. The preferred wedding month for the Amish is October, after the crops have been harvested, but this wedding took place in September. There were only so many Thursdays to go around in the month of October, and with so many young people having weddings in the Holmes County area, September had also become a frequently scheduled wedding month.

Courtship and weddings are not taken lightly by the Amish.

From what I've seen, most Amish people are secretly romantics at heart. From the oldest to the very young, they believe in an endur-ing love between one man and one woman for life. Old women and old men can, and often do, lovingly recount details of their own courtship—even if that courtship took place sixty years ago.

Once, when I was visiting the bride's grandmother as we sat in the living room of the *Daadi Haus,* her little house on the main property, she pointed at a hand-carved wood clock. "Do you see that clock on that shelf on the wall?"

"It's beautiful."

"My husband made that for me before we got married."

"There was a lot of love put into the making of that clock," I remarked.

"*Ja,*" she said, smiling happily. "There was."

When we arrived for the wedding, we were met by Levi, fa-ther of the bride. He was handsome in his new black coat, vest, and pants. With so much responsibility, he was more serious than usual. He politely showed us to the seats they had waiting for us.

The barn, where the actual wedding would be held, was built into the hill, close enough to the house to require only a short walk. The main level of the barn was so clean it practically shined. Brothers and uncles and grandfathers had scrubbed it so well over the past week, there was not so much as a spiderweb in view. Square bales of hay were piled to the rafters along the sides of the barn, as well as in the haymow, to make room for guests. Hang-ing from one beam was a single, perfect hanging basket of blue petunias. It was the only floral decoration in the barn, but it was spectacular.

I wished I could have taken a picture of all of this, but I re-spected my friends' beliefs against the making of graven images.

Instead, I tried to imprint the scene before me on my mind, memorizing details, savoring every moment.

There were three ministers who, taking turns, would preach for nearly three hours by the time this wedding was finished. Everything, as Joyanne had warned, was conducted in German. I recognized a few words—"Noah" and "Moses" and "Abraham"—as the preaching progressed, but the rest of the service was pretty much incomprehensible. This was as it should be. The wedding service was not for me, nor for any of us witnesses, and it was most definitely not for show.

When one preacher got tired, another one took his place. One of them had a sort of singsong cadence to his preaching; another, who was younger, was more impassioned and seemed to hold the crowd's attention a little better. Later I heard comments about what a good speaker he was.

I noticed that the oldest women sat in the back, where even though they were seated on backless benches, they could rest themselves against the wall made of hay. On the men's side, it was different. The old men sat toward the front and the teenage boys sat in the back. It amused me that Amish boys looked about as miserable and bored as most Englisch teenagers would look if expected to sit through three hours of preaching.

Children were sprinkled throughout the group. There is no babysitting service at an Amish church. A little boy who had been sitting with his mother decided that he wanted to go sit with his grandpa. With her permission, he scampered across the open space where the preacher was standing. No one seemed to care. The grandfather, seated up front on the men's side, welcomed his little grandson, who proceeded to run a small toy tractor over his grandfather's knee throughout the rest of the service.

The man fondly patted the little guy's head and went back to listening to the preacher, unconcerned that the child was using him as a runway.

Bride and groom sat together in the front row along with their chosen witnesses. These are usually made up of the bride's best friend or sister, and the groom's best friend or brother. These "side-sitters," along with the bride and groom, do not do anything except listen. This bride was more solemn than I had ever seen her as she absorbed the words of the preacher. She wore a dark navy-blue dress with a white apron, and a black bonnet. This was to emphasize the solemnity of the occasion. After the wedding, she would once again wear the white head covering. She carried no bouquet. Since the Amish do not wear jewelry, there would be no exchange of rings.

Then, suddenly, the whole church rose, turned, and knelt in front of their bench, bowing their heads and engaging in silent prayer. The preacher apparently had given a cue that I did not understand.

This was not the first time I had experienced the Amish way of praying silently even within a group. I don't know why they do this, nor does the husband of one of my Amish friends, whom I asked later. I was used to being "led in prayer" at my church services and at shared meals. My guess is that they believe for one person to attempt to "lead" the prayers for others would be arrogant.

I like their custom of silent prayer. Having allowed my mind to wander too many times during public prayers, I notice that when I am with my Amish friends and left to my own devices to pray in silence for a few moments, I truly do pray.

So, kneeling, I gave thanks for being allowed to be in this

place, at this time, with these good people. I asked God to help me portray their culture accurately and with respect. I also prayed for this young couple, that they would learn early in their marriage the importance of being kind to each other—whether they felt like it or not.

We rose and seated ourselves again. The steady stream of the foreign language lulled me into a pleasant dreamlike state. I was startled when the preaching abruptly ended and the bride and groom stood up. The preacher said a few words directly to them. They answered and nodded, and then suddenly the wedding was over.

The actual wedding ceremony itself, after three hours of preaching, took less than three minutes.

Now that the wedding was over, the feasting and visiting began. Deborah was already rushing around in the cool September weather. Her cheeks were flushed and her eyes were alive with the excitement of hosting this wedding. In spite of having so many other people around, she took time out to make sure Joyanne and I were inside her house and comfortably seated before she rushed off to check on last-minute food preparations.

A few moments later, Mary, who was an aunt of the bride, took me aside. "So, what did you think of the wedding?"

"I enjoyed it, but I only understood about five words," I said. "What were the preachers talking about?"

"They were telling the stories of biblical marriages down through the ages. That's what they do at every wedding," she said.

People began to gravitate toward the large workshop, where tables and benches had been set up. Levi came and ushered me and Joyanne to the correct table. We were among the first to enter and the sight made me gasp. Snowy tablecloths covered long stretches of tables. Golden-colored mint tea glistened in narrow goblets at each place setting. Fresh flowers were positioned at intervals on each table between the lovely dinnerware, along with candles, white netting, and gold-colored ribbons. Sunshine streamed through sparkling windows and winked back at us from the polished silverware.

I was absolutely stunned at the simple, tasteful elegance. This was nothing at all like the church potluck affair set up on sawhorse tables I had envisioned.

Over the years, I have developed a private, extremely judgmental, and nonscientific predictor about marriages. I have a theory that the longer the guests are made to wait for the bride and groom to appear at the reception dinner, the shorter the marriage will last. This hypothesis was developed one Saturday afternoon as I and the other guests waited at the reception for nearly three hours while the bride insisted on a picture-taking marathon, which involved going to several different locations in the city. Her marriage didn't last to their first wedding anniversary.

With no wedding pictures to pose for, it took less than half an hour to get everyone in place. There was a silent prayer. Then food began to arrive. Dish after dish was handed down the long tables family-style as people helped themselves to the bowls and platters of steaming, home-cooked food prepared by the bride's friends and relatives.

Young Amish people glided up and down the aisles, smilingly and competently seeing to everything. I had never seen a professionally catered dinner served as smoothly or as gracefully, and every bite of food was melt-in-your-mouth delicious.

The words to a song had been printed and placed beside each place setting. At some point during the dinner the guests serenaded the couple with what I think was another hymn. Apparently everyone except Joyanne and me was familiar with this song, written in German, and they sang with enthusiasm, the strong voices echoing off the walls.

I was seated at the very end of a long table. A little girl approximately nine or ten years old stood at the end beside me. From what I could tell, her job was to watch and make sure that everyone at our table had everything they needed. She took her responsibility very, very seriously. I noticed that there were other children near her age assigned to each table. In fact, every child over the age of eight seemed to have some small job.

There was a short space of quiet as we concentrated on eating, then a second round of food began. Fresh platters of chicken, dressing, green beans, and baskets of rolls were all carried in from the kitchen and started down the table so everyone could have seconds.

After the meal, everyone was welcome to follow the bride and groom back into the barn, where there was a table set up with gifts. Not everyone participated in this. Most of the men stayed outside and visited. Many of the women were involved in the cleanup. I was anxious to watch, so I went.

I was seated between Joyanne and Frieda, the bride's maternal grandmother. Frieda is one of my favorite people. She is a small, slender woman, and it is hard to imagine her having given birth to twelve children—but it certainly does not seem to have hurt her. She is still as nimble and hardworking as any of her daughters.

As we sat and watched the couple opening their gifts, I noticed a line of six or seven little boys perched upon the top board of a stable, watching. They were all dressed in identical outfits—black pants, black suspenders, white shirts, black hats—all miniatures of their Amish fathers. They reminded me of little birds lined up on a wire. It was obvious from the smiles and whispers that they were enjoying watching the proceedings.

The opening of gifts was different from what I'd observed in Englisch weddings. It appeared that it was traditional for the groom to open each gift and that it was the groom's responsibility to thank the giver. There was no effusive, over-the-top gratitude for an especially nice gift, but merely a dignified nod and thanks. Every gift was equally appreciated. The bride silently read and kept track of the cards. She seemed content to allow him to take the lead.

The gifts were remarkable only for their practicality. There were tools for him, an ironing board and new canning jars for her. A mailbox. A bucket filled with cleaning supplies. A basket of garden tools. A rake, shovel, and hoe tied together with a big bow. A wheelbarrow, a nice barbecue grill, and a garden hose. There was a step stool and a pressure cooker for canning.

Everything that people had deemed necessary to start the young couple off on a good footing was there. They got multiple gifts of the same on-top-of-stove popcorn maker. After they had opened three of these, Frieda leaned toward me and whispered, "I sure do hope they like popcorn!"

Soon, the gifts had all been unwrapped and it was time to leave. Another wave of guests needed to be fed—the young adults who would stay until very late. They would also be served a large meal. The women were already preparing it.

As we said our good-byes, I noticed that the bride and groom were helping with the cleanup. This is expected among the Amish. It would seem arrogant and thoughtless to the family and friends who had worked so hard if the bride and groom simply left.

I learned later that the bridal couple were awake before dawn to help set up for the wedding, and would work until late the night of their wedding. They would spend the night at the bride's home, then get up early the next day to finish taking down the tent and putting everything to rights on the farm. Eventually, when everything was clean and put away, they would load up their gifts to take to their own home.

The bride's parents were pleased with their new son-in-law. He was known as a hard worker and a steady man who would make a good husband and father. Best of all, he was Amish and would help their daughter raise their future grandchildren within their faith.

I can't help but admire the things I saw emphasized that day. Three hours of preaching in which God and His will for marriage were honored. Less than three minutes focused on the bride and groom as they pledged their lifelong commitment to each other. The very firm expectation by everyone there, including the bride and groom, was that the marriage would last for life.

Instead of comments about how beautiful the bride was, I heard people remark upon what a good mother she would make, what a good homemaker she would be. I heard comments about what a hard worker he was, and how well they were suited for each other. In an Amish wedding, there is no drama about wedding dresses. Although the bride always wears a newly made dress, it is not all that different from a regular Amish dress. There is no room for *hochmut* in an Amish wedding. The hundreds or thousands of dollars an Englisch bride might spend on a wedding dress or on decorations for the church are funneled instead into a feast for the guests, many of whom have ridden for hours in rented vans to get there. It is common to see a bride wielding a broom after the guests depart or a groom helping load rented tables and chairs into a van.

Attending an Amish wedding was interesting on several levels, but one of the most striking was the many ways the children were deliberately incorporated into the process, in contrast to some Englisch weddings I attend, where children are not even invited. There was no question here that they were part of the family, and were to be part of making the wedding a success. For instance, as I walked up the driveway with my gift for the couple, several young boys were waiting to relieve guests of their gifts and carry them to the table set up in the barn. My package was heavy, an enameled cast-iron Dutch oven, and I admonished one small boy, about six years old, not to hurt himself as he carried it away. He didn't say a word, just gave me an adorable grin as he hefted it onto his shoulder and then strode off as though to say, "See, lady? I can carry this thing. Just you watch!"

The children were being given small responsibilities throughout the wedding for a reason. They were being taught important principles by example. Amish children, with their large extended families, take part in dozens of weddings before they are adults. As they do so, they observe and soak up core Amish beliefs. They are a willing, helpful part of the community of workers who staff these great events. They also hear the teaching that marriage is to be for life, not only in the words of the preachers, but in the actions and excitement of the adults. They watch the bride and groom serving others by staying to help with the cleanup afterward. They see a large array of close relatives and friends working together in such a way that with so many hands lightening the load, it is not work at all.

Of course, the involvement of children in Amish weddings is

not enough to explain why these children are so well adjusted, but I do think that seeing and hearing over and over how important the family is must have an impact. I'm also convinced that part of the contentment I see in these children stems from the fact that they do not worry about whether the marriages around them will last—they simply assume that they will.

Divorce

"Divorce is not an option."
—QUOTE FROM AMISH WEDDING SERVICE

"You invited yourself to an Amish wedding?" Paul Stutzman laughed when I told him about having attended Rebecca's carefully planned wedding. "That was brave."

"It was *rude*," I said. "I never did find out who gave up their seat for me. I would apologize to them if I knew."

"How did you like sitting there all morning listening to Amish men preaching to you in German? Did you understand any of it?"

"I understood a few words—the names of some of the biblical patriarchs—and one Englisch phrase that kept coming up."

"Really? What phrase was that?"

"'Divorce is not an option.' One of the preachers repeated it three different times in English. Joyanne and I thought maybe he was saying it in English for the benefit of the few Englisch guests there—trying to get it through our thick heads."

"Did you ask anyone if that was the case?"

"Joyanne told me that one of the relatives asked him that very question a few days later, and he said he didn't realize he was doing it."

"I'm not surprised," Paul said. "The idea is taught at every wedding and in every Amish home. Their children are taught by word and deed that marriage is for life."

"But the Amish do divorce, don't they?" I asked.

"Rarely," he said. "Their divorce statistics are less than one percent. The Amish marry for love, but they do not base the longevity of their marriage on romantic love alone. Even if they fall out of love with each other, their values of commitment and dedication to their families help them get through the rough times."

I am certainly no marriage expert, but I'm fairly certain that when an Amish couple gets married, it helps that most have never seen any other kind of marriage modeled except those that last a lifetime. Staying married for life is the Amish norm, not the exception.

Many children of divorced parents with whom I have spoken are determined not to take the same path as their parents. Unfortunately, without healthy marriages as models upon which to base their relationship, staying married is often a greater struggle.

According to researcher Nicholas H. Wolfinger, a phenomenon called the "divorce cycle" kicks in for grown children of divorced parents. Wolfinger, an assistant professor in the University of Utah's Department of Family and Consumer Studies, spent several years studying the children of divorce in America.

His research shows that if one spouse comes from divorced parents, the couple may be up to twice as likely to divorce. Couples who are both children of divorced parents are three times more likely to divorce than couples who have been raised by parents who remained married.

If the idea of a divorce cycle is true, then it stands to reason that the reverse is also true. If one's parents, aunts, uncles, cousins, and grandparents remain married, no doubt it gives young couples a much better model of nurturing lifelong marital relationships.

Another reason for the low divorce rate, Paul informs me, is that if a husband is acting badly toward his wife or children, frequently the leaders of the church will take him to task and hold him accountable for his actions. If he does not do better, they will use shunning to encourage him to make some changes. Amish wives, also, have to face the disapproval of the other women in their close-knit society if they are deficient in caring for their husbands and children. If necessary, the church leaders will insist that the couple get help, pointing to I Corinthians 7:10–11: "To the married I give this command (not I, but the Lord): A wife must not separate from her husband. But if she does, she must remain unmarried or else be reconciled to her husband. And a husband must not divorce his wife." Some Amish churches go to great lengths to keep troubled marriages together.

I personally know of one Amish marriage in which the husband had some severe emotional issues. There were also two handicapped children in the family, which placed a great strain on the marriage. The leaders of that particular Amish church made certain that the husband was taken to a Mennonite-run facility for in-house counseling, while two other Amish families volunteered to care for the handicapped children until the mother and father could work out their problems.

While the father was living at the counseling center and unable to work, the church supported the mother financially as well as emotionally. The last I heard, that family is functioning again after taking a lengthy breather from one another. I was impressed with the intimate involvement of the members of that Old Order Amish religious community in trying to keep this family intact.

Because of the close-knit nature of an Amish church, where the maximum number a church might have is approximately two hundred people, it becomes harder to keep marital problems private. Although an Amish man or woman is more likely to trust and go to an older member of their church for advice than to see a professional marriage counselor, sometimes that advice is wise enough to have an impact.

Once, an Amish woman with ten stair-step children confided to me that she had been unsure what to do when her babies kept coming year after year. Money was tight, and her husband had to take on extra work to support them. She was exhausted from childbirth and felt unable to give the children that she already had the care that they needed.

Instead of going to a clinic, a doctor, or a church leader for advice, or even a family member, she went to an older, wiser Amish woman in her church and privately discussed the issue of birth control. She wanted to know if she was doing something wrong in the eyes of the church if she limited her family. The older woman's counsel was that it should be a decision made between husband and wife—not something for church leaders to decide.

The fact that an older Amish woman had basically given her permission to use some form of birth control gave the younger woman peace. She said, because of that, she did not feel at all guilty when she and her husband privately made the decision to try not to have any more children.

What was interesting to me about this conversation is that the older woman's advice had such weight. From what I can see, one of the first lines of defense in an Amish marriage is the older people from within their church who have already been through it and figured some things out.

Are their marriages perfect? No. But because Amish couples go into marriage determined to stay together, they work a lot harder at forgiving and loving one another when tough times come.

In contrast, I once received a phone call from a young Englisch woman, telling me about her engagement. I was pleased for her until she said something that worried me a great deal.

"He says he'll make me happy," she said. "And I want to be happy."

The marriage barely made it past the honeymoon.

The expectations the Amish have about marriage tend to be a little different from Englisch expectations. Although they marry for love, they do not marry expecting their spouse to make them "happy." Happiness in marriage is seen by the Amish as a by-product of a godly life, not a goal in itself.

There is a book that's been out for a while with the wonderful title *What If God Designed Marriage to Make Us Holy More than to Make Us Happy?* I've mentioned this title to a couple of Amish friends, who have chuckled and nodded their heads with enthusiasm. Yes, they laugh. That is quite possible. Some marriages do tend to make some people a whole lot more holy than happy.

No one would argue against the proposition that long-lasting, loving marriages have a positive impact on children. In the Amish mind-set, that is the most critical thing of all to consider. Even an Amish man or woman who finds themselves wishing they had not married the person they are married to is likely to try to find a way to stay the course and be content.

"When we marry," one Amish minister tells me, "we don't just get married because we think we are in love. Loving feelings can come and go. Instead, we commit ourselves to that other person for life, and we are a people who are taught from childhood on up to honor our commitments."

This Amish philosophy was brought home to me the day Paul was reading through the contract he had to sign with the publisher before we began writing this book. The contract was lengthy and complicated. Publishers take a risk when they hire writers, and need to cover all their bases if something goes wrong. A publishing contract can be a little intimidating.

"What do you think?" I asked Paul after we'd both taken the time to read through it. "Are you going to sign this?"

"Sure. I'll sign, but what they don't realize is that it really doesn't matter if I sign or not. I live by the same philosophy that my father and my grandfather lived by."

I'm aware that his grandfather was a well-respected bishop in the Amish church and I was interested to hear this philosophy.

"And what is that?"

Paul signed and initialed the pages. "If I tell someone I'll do something—I do it."

Years ago, when my husband was in seminary, we lived in a big old house on campus that had been divided into three apartments. The back porch was the entryway into our apartment, and out-side—where a flower bed had once stood—my husband created a large sandbox for our son, who was about three years old. That sandbox and the toys we kept there became a magnet for neighbor-hood children, most of whom belonged to other seminary students.

One day, about a week before graduation, the two little girls who lived in the apartment at the front of the house were playing in the sandbox. The elder, who was about six, was prattling on to me about her daddy's new church where they were going to be moving in a few days.

During this conversation, the little girl said something I've never forgotten—nor has my husband, who overheard it.

"My daddy says that when we get to our new house he'll build me a sandbox just like this one . . ." She used a little bulldozer to make tracks in the sand. "And if my daddy says he will build me a sandbox, I *know* he will because my daddy always keeps his promises."

The thing that got to me wasn't just the statement—which was powerful enough—it was the matter-of-fact, contented way in which the little girl said it. That child had total confidence that a sandbox would soon appear in her future for no other reason than that she had a father who kept his promises.

The little girl was right. I knew her dad. He was a man of integrity. If he said he would do something, you could count on him to do it, and that fact made his daughter's world a very safe and stable place.

In a world that seems to be in constant turmoil, a child's need for adults who keep their promises and provide stability is greater than ever before.

I am aware that many parents may not have the option of providing the kind of home environment that little girl had, with two parents who loved each other. On the other hand, a family counselor I spoke with recently emphasized the fact that even if a marriage or home is falling apart, children can survive emotionally if there is at least one or two adults in their lives who choose to provide some stability for them.

"Grandparents often underestimate the impact they have on a child," he said. "As do aunts, uncles, friends—just one or two people in a child's life they know they can trust and count on will make a huge difference in the kind of person they become."

In other words, it is no small thing to become a keeper of promises in a child's life—even if one is not the biological parent.

The Role of the Extended Family

"It already felt like home."
—AMISH GRANDFATHER

Each time Paul and I discuss the research I'm doing for this book, I notice that Paul will bring his Amish grandparents into the conversation. I don't think this is intentional; it is just that they hold such a large place in his childhood memories, and so they are often on his mind. He recounts the many board games they enjoyed at his grandmother's kitchen table. He describes how he and his cousins were allowed to practice throwing a knife into a chunk of wood inside his grandparents' home in the wintertime when he and his cousins couldn't go outside to play, and he shakes his head in awe over the fact that his grandmother allowed it.

He also tells about her assigning him chores whenever he was staying with her, and how much he did not want to do those chores . . . but did so anyway. His grandmother was a woman who thoroughly enjoyed her grandchildren, but expected them to be obedient and saw to it that they knew how to work. It is easy to see that much of Paul's integrity and work ethic were formed not only by his parents but also by his grandparents during frequent visits to their farm.

Paul is not alone in this. I've noticed that there is a greater tendency among people from Amish backgrounds to include stories about their grandparents in our conversations than when I talk with my Englisch friends. I do not believe this is accidental. It is obvious that grandparents loom large in the life of Amish-raised children.

Two reasons for this strike me as I spend time with various Amish families. Most Amish homes have what the Englisch would call a "mother-in-law apartment," but the Amish refer to it with the more pleasing term *Daadi Haus* (grandfather's house). This is a much smaller, separate home loosely connected to the larger family house by a porch, a connecting door, or a short walkway. This small home solves many problems.

The Amish, unless completely infirm, don't ever really retire. For instance, my friends Joe and Elizabeth sold a portion of their farm, including the house in which they had reared their eleven children, to their daughter and son-in-law. At that point, the older couple, now in their early seventies, moved into the *Daadi Haus* a few feet away.

The daughter and her husband make payments on the farm, which provides a base of income for Joe and Elizabeth, who do not receive Social Security (the Amish do not, as a rule). The son-in-law is a hard worker and a good farmer. When harvesttime comes, Joe, a healthy seventy-two, helps out with the harvest and other work around the farm. The son-in-law is grateful for his father-in-law's help and expertise.

Joe is a kind man who loves his children and grandchildren. He recently began a small business with one of his daughters to supplement both their incomes. Together they design and sell harnesses for all sorts of domestic animals.

I asked Joe if moving into the *Daadi Haus* had been a hard transition for him.

"No," he said. "I built it with my own hands many years ago, when my own parents were in need of a smaller house. It already felt like home to me."

In the meantime, Elizabeth helps her grown daughters with all sorts of food preparation. The first time I met her, she was busily sorting peaches in her daughter's next-door basement kitchen. They had plans to preserve enough peaches to get both families through the winter.

Elizabeth, when the peach-sorting was finished, was kind enough to invite me over to tour her *Daadi Haus*. Two of her daughter's young children trailed along behind us—curious as always about an Englisch guest.

I was impressed with the gleaming woodwork, oak cabinets, and solid wood floors. The two bedrooms and sitting room were all small, but the kitchen was large. The table alone was big enough to handle the lunch she was planning later for her five daughters, several grandchildren, and me.

The relationships between her and her daughters was warm and laced with laughter. Grandchildren often ran in and out.

For now, Joe and Elizabeth are healthy and viable. They are obviously helping their daughter and son-in-law raise the children, can the food, and run the farm. But all of them know that there will come a time when they will be able to do less and less. There will come a time when they will need help.

When that day comes, the *Daadi Haus* will become the Amish answer to an assisted living home, and eventually the

Amish answer to a nursing home as other members of the family also come to help. Amish elderly do not end up in nursing homes. With their large, close-knit families, it seems there is almost always a family member willing to care for aging parents. The fact that most women do not work outside their home facilitates this.

There are many benefits to the grandparents living close. Amish children are taught to respect their grandparents—and with good reason. Joe is a spiritual man and faithful to the precepts of the Old Order Amish church. He has much he can teach them, and not all of it is about farming. They are already great-grandparents to a new baby, and after raising eleven children, Elizabeth is a fount of information about childhood sicknesses and raising babies. From what I could see, her knowledge and advice is eagerly received by her daughters and granddaughters.

I admire the easy camaraderie I watch between Elizabeth and her children and grandchildren. This is a hardworking, supportive, and loving family. Elizabeth obviously enjoys being surrounded by her grandchildren, but—she confides as she shows me around the lovely *Daadi Haus*—it's nice to have a place where she can get away from them every once in a while.

Making certain the elderly within an Amish family know they are cared for is a high priority, even for those grown children who do not have the grandparents living next door. When discussing the need to care for their elderly, Psalm 71:9 is sometimes cited: "Do not cast me away when I am old; do not forsake me when my strength is gone."

One of the men I talked with described how he and his wife made an "intentional" decision about keeping the family close. His mother lives in a *Daadi Haus* attached to his sister's home, but he makes sure their family spends an entire Sunday with her at least once a month.

"She's widowed," he explains, "and needs to know she can depend on that time with us."

I can almost guarantee that when his time comes, his children, having been taught such thoughtful kindness by his example, will make certain that he will be able to depend on them as well to take time to be with him.

Many of us do not have the option of living near close relatives because our jobs keep us hundreds or thousands of miles away. And sometimes living far away is a conscious decision, made for the sake of the children or one's own sanity. If there are toxic or abusive relatives in one's life, it is good parenting not to subject ourselves and our children to them.

On the other hand, sometimes the decision is an arbitrary one and needs to be reexamined. When my husband and I moved away, our parents were still relatively young and healthy and able to drive to wherever we were living. We took them to museums, various tourist attractions, and my father-in-law joked that they didn't take vacations—they just came to visit us and saved lots of money.

Then both of our fathers died, our mothers were widowed, and since we came from the same hometown, we decided to move back to the rural home area we grew up in to be available to them. The move involved a pay cut, but we believed it would be worth it, and it was.

Our sons got to finish growing up among their extended family, and they still value that they have so many good memories of those who have since passed. Not having to drive all those hours to get home on holidays was quite a bonus to all of us. Getting to stay in our own home instead of toting kids and presents hundreds of miles made Christmas an enjoyable experience instead of drudgery. The pay cut was made up for by living within a network of helpful relatives who were willing to share what they had with us. It was not necessary, for instance, to buy a ladder when my brother-in-law had one he wasn't using. My sister, an organic gardener, shared home-grown produce with us, and appreciated the fact that I helped shoulder the responsibilities of caring for our aged mother.

Our sons also knew that they were growing up in a small community where practically everyone knew them and/or was related to them. They knew that if their behavior got out of hand, there was a strong possibility that one of the relatives would see it, and make sure to let us know about it. There was also the reassurance that if anything happened, help was not far away. As we look back at the pros and cons, we still feel that the benefits of eventually moving near our extended family far outweighed the financial sacrifice. Providing roots can sometimes be important enough to the well-being of one's family that it is worth the personal sacrifice of moving closer if at all possible.

What if it isn't possible? A wise parent should try to find some decent and kind people who'll stand in as surrogate family. An elderly Hispanic neighbor called herself Grandma Rachel to my boys until the day she died. We lived in a neighborhood of small homes set close together and I knew she kept an eagle eye out for my kids. She was a wonderful friend to our family and we cherished her.

Of course, all the new technology has made it possible to stay more emotionally connected even when we don't live close to one another. Skype was a wonderful tool for my son and his family when he was serving in Afghanistan. My granddaughter tells me their face-to-face nightly talks on Skype helped her feel like he wasn't so far away.

It takes a little more effort, and maybe the investment of some financial resources in travel or technology, but it is worth the time to develop these intergenerational bonds. A sense of caring family, even if that family is a thousand miles away, is still important for a child's sense of who they are and to whom they belong. Even the Amish sometimes have to live far apart, but they value the importance of family so much they will go to great efforts to visit one another and stay in touch. If nothing else, the Amish have taught me that enduring family ties are more necessary to children than many of us ever realized.

Eating Together

"Unless we have at least one meal together as a family—
the day does not feel right."
—AMISH MOTHER

All this insistence on family and intentionally making family the center of life has some broad-reaching implications for how Amish children see the world and their place in it. But the importance of family for the Amish has other, more tangible benefits as well, at least in the everyday lives of mothers with small children.

I realized this one evening when I was having dinner with my friend Leah's family. We were having a nice conversation, but suddenly I realized that there was something missing from our conversation. We were surrounded by her young children, but never once did I hear her tell her children to eat their food. She makes very healthy meals, and is knowledgeable about health and nutrition. The whole-grain bread, for instance, had been made from non-GMO wheat that she orders from a company out west. Yet, in spite of her concern about nutrition, and in spite of the fact that she was unabashedly setting out wheat bread, not the processed white bread that is all most of the children I know will touch, I have never heard her say to one of her children, "Eat that, it's good for you!"

Unfortunately, when my boys were small, I made this comment a *lot*. As a young mother, I was obsessed with getting the right amount of calories and nutrition into their little bodies, and as I look back, I think I pretty much drove everyone nuts with it.

My eldest son still shudders when he talks about the pasta with spinach mixed into the noodles that I sent to school in his lunch. The other kids made fun of his "green spaghetti," so of course he went hungry rather than eat it in front of them. For a while I secretly blended cooked zucchini into spaghetti sauce, until one of the boys caught me at it and tattled to his brothers. Then there was the homemade whole wheat bread I labored over that was so heavy and dense even I couldn't force myself to eat it. I'm the only woman I know who has made her own tofu from scratch. My sons hated it, and still do.

I thought I had really stumbled onto something when, instead of what I thought was unhealthy white-flour commercial saltines, I tried to entice my kids into eating homemade tomato soup by putting out a bowl of popcorn to sprinkle into it. I thought my youngest was especially fond of that dish until he confessed that his older brother was secretly rewarding him for each spoonful by handing him a baseball card under the table. It worked well until he realized that they were his *own* baseball cards, which his brother had filched from his stash.

When I worked as a teacher's aide, I saw a few other mothers who were even more focused on nutrition than I was. One was so determined that her children never taste refined sugar that she sent a modified, whole-grain, healthier version of cupcakes to school every time there was a birthday party, so her daughter would have something healthy to eat. I felt vaguely inferior to her until I discovered her child was tossing her mother's "good" cupcakes into the trash and eating the fancy, sugar-filled birthday cupcakes that all the other children were enjoying.

Therefore, I was extremely impressed when, with no fanfare or discussion, Leah's children happily ate the food she passed around the table—vegetables, whole grains, and all. As I sat there, I realized that I had never heard an Amish child complain about not liking the food that had been set before them. I'm sure it happens. I'm just saying I've never heard it.

At a larger event, I had seen more than a dozen small Amish children file through a potluck food line without once complaining about the food choices. I also didn't see parents hovering over them worriedly asking if their child wanted a piece of this, a spoonful of that. The parents seemed to take it for granted that their children would accept the food placed in front of them, and the children seemed to take it for granted, too.

I asked Leah about this later, and at first she seemed puzzled by the idea that a child might refuse to eat the good food they were given. But when I pressed her about it, she offered as a possible explanation the fact that the Amish place a deliberate emphasis on sharing meals as a family.

Leah's husband gets up early for work, while it is still dark. One morning while I was staying with them, I was stumbling to the bathroom with a flashlight in my hand, passed the kitchen, and caught a glimpse of Leah sitting at the kitchen table, keeping her husband company as he ate his breakfast.

They were talking softly together beneath the glow of a gaslight. Leah had not fixed a labor-intensive breakfast. She had not been rushing around frying bacon or scrambling eggs. Instead, her husband was spooning up a large bowl of the homemade granola she had baked the day before, and she was enjoying some time with him before he left.

This was their time together and I did not interrupt.

At six o'clock, after her husband had gone, I saw her getting the children up.

I noted that the children ate together and each had a few indoor and outdoor chores to finish before Leah began their schoolwork. Though she had the option of sending them to the Amish school down the road, she had chosen instead to homeschool all her children.

"Why?" I asked.

"I just enjoy having the time with them," she answered.

The children did their schoolwork under their mother's oversight while I got some work done on my battery-operated laptop.

Lunch was a simple affair with her, me, and the younger children together at the table.

"Is there anything you don't like to eat?" I asked the eight-year-old.

"I don't like wild rice very much," she answered.

"So—if you came to my house, and I served wild rice, what would you do?"

She looked at her mother for help on how to deal with the question.

"She would probably whisper something about it to me," Leah said. "And I would ask her to eat a little of it anyway."

"And would you?" I asked the child.

She nodded.

"Even though you don't like it, you would eat it anyway?"

"I would try very hard to eat some of it," she said.

This began a discussion among the four children about food preferences. I found out that they had stronger opinions about food than I had suspected. They all mentioned things they didn't necessarily enjoy, but all agreed that their preferences would not keep them from eating that particular food item if it were placed in front of them.

Later that evening, when we gathered around the supper table, Leah was visibly worried because an older son's work kept him too late to sit down and eat with the rest of us.

"It's so important for a family to eat together," she told me. "As the children get older, schedules change and we aren't able to have every meal together, but we try to make sure to have at least one each day when everyone is present. If we don't . . . things just do not feel right to me."

As the dishes were passed around, I noticed that individual children took more of some food than others, but they all ate some of each dish. There wasn't a lot of discussion about the food, but there was a lively discussion about the goat auction we planned to go to the next day.

Leah's meals are always wholesome and tasty, but they aren't elaborate. The phrase *comfort food* came to mind as I sat at the table with them, but I don't think the comfort necessarily comes from the food alone. The comfort comes from the company. This was a family who liked each other and enjoyed having a guest as well.

Like everyone else, I have favorite dishes. When I think about those dishes, much of my enjoyment comes from the social associations with them that I remember. The first curry dish I ever tasted was at the home of a family who had done mission work in Africa. As I sat at that table hearing interesting stories about their time in that country, I decided that I liked curry very much indeed.

I disliked potato soup as a child, until my mother became very ill and was unable to care for me for several days. I remember my aunt showing up with a pot of potato soup, plopping me down on her lap, and spooning it down me without asking whether or not I liked it—while she scolded my mother for not calling her sooner.

I remember being relieved that someone was finally taking care of me and being surprised that potato soup could taste so good. My aunt's recipe was exactly like my mother's, but the relief and gratitude I felt about her showing up made it a favorite comfort food from that point on. I actually crave it when I'm unwell, even today.

If I think back, nearly all my favorite foods have a story attached involving other people whom I loved or were kind to me.

Eating real food with our children, on a daily basis, without turning a meal into a battlefield, isn't a magical answer to childhood pickiness, but I think it is a factor, especially if the food does not become the focus of the conversation.

"It also helps if the parents train themselves not to be picky eaters in front of their children," Mary once pointed out. "John is not fond of tomatoes, but he eats them in front of the children anyway."

Another factor that leads Amish children to eat what's put in front of them is that the Amish tend to raise a great deal of their own food, usually with children tagging along and helping. I've noticed that if children are involved in the preparation of food, they are much more likely to try new things. Doing even just a small part of the harvesting of fruits and vegetables will tempt them to be more adventurous about trying new foods.

My eight-year-old grandson was opposed to tasting any kind of fruit except apples until he was visiting one day and helped me pick pears. The activity of picking ripe pears straight off the tree in my backyard was intriguing enough that he finally ventured a taste. Before long, he was sitting beside me in the grass, munching the fresh fruit like a veteran fruit eater. In fact, he loved pears so much that they became one of his favorite foods and for quite a while, he had to have a pear for breakfast every morning.

Amish children have this sort of experience almost daily throughout the various seasons. Even in the late winter, they help their mother plant seeds in containers on window sills, and in early spring they make a trip to a nursery for seedlings. Preparing the soil, planting, weeding, checking the first carrot, rejoicing over the first tomato, being amazed at the abundance of a few zucchini plants, or being allowed to have their own allotted garden space to grow watermelons, as Paul Stutzman told me he did as a child— all this has an effect on their appetites and food preferences.

Not everyone has enough earth to plant a large garden, but something as simple as helping a child plant a container of cherry tomatoes on a patio can pique their interest. It is hard not to want to taste what one has nurtured and helped to harvest.

I write about this as though I know how to garden, but the truth is, I'm an abysmal gardener. I always have such good intentions, but I forget to water, or I accidentally use the wrong fertilizer, or I get an infestation of worms that eat up the cabbage plants. The spirit is willing, but the skill is lacking, and the enthusiasm I had in spring wanes drastically about mid-July.

But even my imperfect attempts brought about enough of a harvest to be interesting to my sons when they were children. There might have been only two tomatoes, but we revered those two tomatoes that year. One summer I attempted watermelons. Only one watermelon survived, and we ran outside each morning to see how much it had grown. Excitement ran high when we finally sliced into it.

A parent doesn't have to be a master gardener to give children at least some of the experience of harvesting food. Pick-your-own fruit orchards offer activities most children enjoy. It is a rare child who doesn't want to sample the ripe blueberries he picked all by himself. One of our favorite things to do when we lived in Michigan was to drive north and pick ripe sweet cherries. The picking involved actually climbing into low-hanging trees, a perfect opportunity for an active child to work off some energy. Visits to a cherry orchard and the fun of eating sweet black cherries in the backseat of our car made cherries one of my sons' favorite foods.

Another thing my sons enjoyed when we lived in the city was making a trip to the farmers' market each Saturday. Purchasing produce straight from the farmer who grew it and had just pulled it from the earth was a form of harvest in itself as well as an adventure.

I believe that the further children get away from the earth and the process of planting, watering, and harvesting, the less interested they will be in eating real food. They will naturally default back to the highly processed junk food that they see in commercials.

Of course, all these issues are so much less prevalent in Amish families, and not just because they grow much of their own food but because of the lack of television in their lives. As I've spoken to other mothers and grandmothers, I've become more and more convinced that my theory—though it's a highly unscientific theory based on my own personal experience—has merit.

I was in first grade before our family bought a television. I remember seldom thinking about food up to that point except to enjoy it whenever mealtime came around. We rarely snacked unless the apples on the tree in the backyard were ripe, or sometimes I would wander out into the tomato patch with a salt shaker in hand and surfeit myself with sun-warmed garden tomatoes if I was hungry and dinner wasn't ready.

I remember the very first time I realized that I was actually *craving* something specific. I was watching my first Kraft food commercial. The buttery voice-over of the narrator and the vision of that creamy Kraft mayonnaise being spooned into a bowl was heady stuff to a six-year-old. Commercial mayonnaise was not something my mother ever bought, but I saw it on television and I wanted some.

There were also the sugary-cereal commercials that suddenly appeared in our home, where breakfast usually involved foods like oatmeal with honey, fresh-caught fish, fried potatoes, scrambled eggs, or homemade bread covered with wild blackberry jam.

Once we got a television, I suddenly wanted a breakfast that matched the jingle in a commercial ("Snap, crackle, pop . . . Rice Krispies!"), especially if there was the promise of a toy inside the box. Things changed in our home when the television appeared, and that was no accident. It was a well-planned campaign by food companies to make a profit, and it worked.

According to the Nielsen Corporation, food products and fast-food restaurants are ranked number one in the type of TV advertisements marketed during kids' programming, and Nielsen also estimates that American children watch approximately 20,000 thirty-second commercials per year.

Food companies pay billions of dollars for a few minutes of commercial airtime during children's programming, and there is a good reason for this: commercials have a profound effect. Well-funded, well-researched ads tell children what they should eat and where they should eat it. Research has proven that television commercials have a much greater effect on children's food choices than do their parents' preferences or suggestions.

In other words, there are extremely well orchestrated reasons that our children beg for unhealthy food or refuse to eat anything but Chicken McNuggets, but these reasons have little to do with a growing child's need for good nutrition. And, as any parent realizes when they have had to pull their child off the ceiling after a birthday party involving too much sugar, bad nutrition can cause bad behavior.

The Amish are not forbidden to eat junk food, but in the homes I've visited, junk food is rare. The Amish are not forbidden to stop at fast-food restaurants, but eating at them is not a way of life. It isn't exactly "fast food" if one has to hitch up a horse and buggy to get there. I've also never seen anything on the table to drink except water or milk. There was lemonade once for a special family dinner, but that is rare. The children seem well satisfied with these two simple beverages.

I think another factor is that Amish children have physical chores to accomplish each day, and with no video games and television to keep them on the couch, they tend to be much more physically active. I think the enthusiasm Amish children show for real food might sometimes have a lot to do with the simple fact that they actually have an appetite when they come to the table.

Having an appetite is no small thing when it comes to pickiness. I saw this played out at our church one weekend. Our youth director observed a thirty-six-hour "lock-in" during which the teenagers voluntarily ate nothing except some water and juice. The goal was to raise awareness of world hunger. The pocket money they saved by not eating out would go to a local homeless shelter.

They were to break their fast with chicken-and-rice soup, which I was asked to supply. I didn't have a recipe for such a large group, so it was a little bit of this and a lot of that, and a little more broth and some vegetables, and finally I had a huge pot of soup—but as I looked at the hodgepodge of chicken, broth, rice, broccoli, carrots, and peas, I realized I'd made a huge mistake.

It tasted great, but it looked—even to me—like slop, and I knew no self-respecting teenager in our church would eat it. I knew these kids. I'd cooked for these kids before. I'd seen them turn their noses up at much better-looking foods than this pot of soup.

But time was short, the soup was all I had, and I discovered that after thirty-six hours without solid food, there *were* no picky eaters in the teen group. Not one. They lined up with their bowls in their hands, and I have never fed such a grateful group of people. There was not one complaint. Every teen came back, humbly asking for seconds. And—I thought this was hilarious—a few days afterward I started getting requests from various mothers for my "wonderful" soup recipe because their teenager kept raving about how delicious it was.

Am I recommending starving a child? Absolutely not! But I will say that I seldom see Amish children snack between meals. I haven't even seen them ask permission to have a snack, except once, when I brought a box of fancy chocolate to Leah's house as a gift and the littlest child asked for a piece. The elder sister graciously accepted the gift and put it on a high shelf for "later." The thing that surprised me was that the youngest child did not fuss or throw a tantrum, but calmly accepted the older sister's pronouncement. Snacking was not something they were used to, so it wasn't an issue.

Maybe the difficulties so many parents face in getting their children to eat at meals could be helped by intentionally making snacks inaccessible, and by encouraging their children to work up their appetites doing things outdoors like taking a long walk or playing. Allowing a child to work up a real appetite and then simply sitting down as a family to eat certainly works for the Amish.

No one wants to fight with their children. It's so much easier to give in, and believe me, I understand how and why it happens. But I also believe that sometimes it is worth making some changes. It isn't wise or kind to allow children to grow up on junk simply because it's easier to cave in to them than to encourage habits that lead to healthy eating.

However, there is one notable exception to this—even in Amish families.

"What about grandparents?" I asked Mary. "I'll bet Amish grandparents don't give children junk food either. Right?"

"Oh, you would be wrong about that." She laughs. "John's mother says she enjoys giving our children lots of candy when they are at her house and then sending them home mad. She also makes sure there are always potato chips or cookies available for them at her house."

"And you are okay with this?" I asked.

"Of course I am." Mary seemed surprised I would ask. "She is their grandmother."

In other words, there are some ways in which there is absolutely no difference at all between our two cultures.

The Importance of Gender Roles

"Together we do whatever is necessary to care for our family."

—AMISH MOTHER WHEN ASKED HOW SHE
AND HER HUSBAND DIVIDE HOUSEHOLD TASKS

Before I met my Amish friends, I had a lot of preconceived ideas about Amish women. I expected them to be downtrodden and abused by overwork. I expected to find a male-dominated society in which women's needs and dreams were ignored. How could a woman who was constantly enduring the drudgery of giving birth and caring for large numbers of children have any life of her own? Let alone ever be happy?

Instead, the Amish women I met seemed to experience more peace and contentment and even, surprisingly, have more free time than many of the overwhelmed and frantic young Englisch women I knew. Though most Amish mothers have at least five and some have seven or more children, they tend to spend more time than their Englisch counterparts in various craft and leisure activities. I believe there are a couple of things that factor into this.

In my experience, some of the feeling of being overwhelmed with responsibilities that so many Englisch women deal with has less to do with the actual crush of work than with data overload and social isolation.

We can read and assimilate more useless information in a half hour online than our great-grandmothers did in a year. In one fifteen-minute scroll through Facebook today, I saw a homeless child huddling in a box in Afghanistan, a badly abused dog, and yet another example of what appears to be nearly suicidal stupidity on the part of our government.

In fifteen minutes I grieved over the child, wept over the dog, and felt angry over the governmental issue.

I am not at all sure it was necessary for me to consume all that information and pain with my morning coffee—especially since I cannot help that child, have never abused an animal, and have little control over what goes on in Washington.

I think we have become so used to being bombarded with all this information that it creates more emotional pressure on us than we realize, especially since too much of it—particularly what we watch on the news and consider the "real" world—is of the sky-is-falling variety.

Much of the rest of the informational barrage involves ways to improve ourselves, our bodies, our clothes, our hair, our health, our teeth, our food, our marriages, our careers, and our finances. Inherent in all that advice is, of course, the assumption that there is something terribly wrong with us that needs fixing.

An Amish woman, on the other hand, usually gets her information and advice from asking another woman face-to-face, talking with her husband, catching a ride to the nearest public library, or reading her latest copy of *Family Life*, an Amish monthly magazine.

I'm familiar with *Family Life* magazine because Naomi, one

of my Amish friends, has loaned me a few of her copies. It's put out by Pathway Publishers of Aylmer, Ontario, and is a homey, chatty publication primarily created for the Plain community that has practical articles about parenting, living a Christian life, medical advice, and anything else the editors think might enhance the quality of a home. The tone is hopeful and encouraging. It often reminds me of the conversations I hear among my Amish women friends. From what I've observed, much of the contentment I see in my Amish friends' lives is based on an incredibly active and nurturing social life. In addition to all-day worship and lunch every other Sunday, there always seems to be a tea or work frolic or quilting or fund-raising dinner for them to attend.

Amish women seldom even go shopping alone. They believe it is more fun and definitely more frugal if one is hiring a van to invite plenty of other women to share the cost.

"Amish women don't just ride in our vans," Clay told me while recounting his experiences as a driver. "They bring a picnic and make a party out of it. Most of the time they pass some of their homemade baked goods up to us, too."

"I'll bet you don't mind that," I said.

"It's a nice perk." He grinned happily. "Amish women are good cooks."

"I'll amen that!" Joyanne said. "Want to hear an Amish joke about their practice of hiring a driver?"

"Sure."

"Do you know how many Amish women you can get into a van?"

"No."

Joyanne mischievously held up a finger. "Just one more."

I didn't quite get the joke, so Clay explained. "If at all possible, they always seem to find room for one more person. If it weren't for making sure everyone has a seat belt, I don't know how many friends and cousins they might try to pack into our vans. They are most definitely a sociable people."

Without a steady diet of movies, television shows, and Hollywood personalities—with only one another to compare themselves to—the women have a more realistic acceptance of their body image. Amish women and teenage girls don't compare themselves to professional models and actresses. Nor do the men compare their wives and girlfriends to impossible airbrushed standards. A woman who is a good manager, a good mother, a good cook, and obedient to God is a prize in the Amish culture—and best of all, she knows it.

Still, as I talked to my Amish friends about their parenting, I had been dreading asking about one thing. I had been in enough Amish homes to know that in general, men go to work, while women stay home and raise the kids and cook and clean. I assumed that strictly defined gender roles would be part of what I was told about how Amish families operated. I also knew how some of my Englisch friends—especially younger women—felt about what they perceived as outdated and sexist definitions of what men and women's roles should be. I was wary of stepping into that minefield, but when I finally worked up the courage to ask Mary how gender roles work in their family, I was more than a little surprised by what she had to say.

"A lot of people think the Amish have very specific gender roles," I explained to her. "And that it is restrictive to women. Do you feel like you and John have ever had problems over who does what in your marriage?"

"Do you mean like if I wanted to go work in the fields with him?" she said. "Or work in the barn like him?"

"Yes."

"You know me, Serena." She smiled. "I'm surprised you would need to even ask. Some people might think it is man's work, but I *love* being outside, working in the fields, planting and harvesting. I enjoy working in the barn with our animals, too. I always have."

"And John doesn't mind?"

"John likes it. He enjoys having me helping him. We work well together no matter what the task. We always have."

"But John would never take on your domestic chores," I said. "Like cooking. I mean, an Amish man would never do that, would he?"

"Of course he would, and John does."

"John can cook?" I was amazed. "You must mean something simple like making a sandwich or something, right?"

"No. John is a very *good* cook," she insisted. "Not just basic things. He can make about anything you want to name. He is an excellent cook."

This was the first time she had ever managed to shock me. John is quite masculine. The image of him whipping up cake batter is hard to imagine.

"How on earth did John learn how to cook?"

"His mother taught him. She taught all her sons how to cook, but John is probably the best. It came in very handy when I was having babies, or when I've been ill. John has always been able to take good care of me and the children."

"Okay, so cooking is not out of the question, but an Amish man would never sew, would he?"

"John has not needed to learn, but I have known some Amish men who do," she said. "In fact, I know of one Amish man who helps his wife make their entire living by both of them sewing. They have two sewing machines and she taught him how."

"Really?"

"Amish husbands and wives, in general, simply do whatever is necessary to take care of their family."

I thought this over. How many of the Englisch couples I know could say the same? I know there are fathers who stay home with their children, and some who cook and clean, but did I personally know of any who would take a full-time job sewing? I couldn't think of any.

"But what about church?" I asked.

"What about it?"

"The Amish church doesn't allow women to preach or take a leadership role. How do you feel about that?"

"Why would I want to take on that kind of responsibility?" Mary blinked in surprise. "Church is one of the few times I get a chance to sit down and *rest*."

I smothered a laugh. Her opinion might not be politically correct, but it was most definitely heartfelt.

"What about financial decisions? Does John take care of the money or do you?"

"We usually make the big decisions together. With the smaller decisions we trust each other to make good ones." Her brow creased. "It isn't a matter of deciding what you call gender roles, at least not in this household. It is about helping one another when help is needed. It is also about respecting each other's strengths. I respect him as a man, and as the spiritual head of our household. I think many Englisch women don't seem to understand how badly their husbands *need* to be respected. He respects me as a woman and as the mother of his children. Together we do whatever is necessary to care for our family."

I hear the truth behind what she's saying, and I've seen this played out in the other Amish households I've visited. One of the ironies about what I have heard described as a male-dominated society is that in general, Amish husbands seem to value and respect their wives a good deal more than Englisch husbands. The little put-downs that some Englisch husbands like to do, the "harmless" teasing, the complaints about women in general that come out of some Englisch men's mouths—those things just aren't part of an Amish husband's conversation.

Paul Stutzman validates this. He says he, too, has observed down through the years the fact that Amish men treat their wives with more respect than do many Englisch men. He believes that the high value they place on family life probably causes them to respect the work a woman does and be more appreciative of the responsibilities she carries.

I saw this respect shown in a small but telling way while visiting my midwife friend, Grace. It had been a hard week for her. She had assisted with several births, but our time together was short, and there was much she wanted to tell me. She was not a young woman, and the work was getting harder for her.

"Will you please make me a cup of mint tea?" she asked her husband.

"Of course." Henry jumped up, solicitous. "Are your poor feet hurting again?"

She admitted that they were.

I watched as he went to a great deal of trouble to make the tea. He punched up the woodstove, filled a teakettle, put it on to boil, went outside, gathered some fresh mint, crushed it, made the tea, and brought it to her, a worried expression on his face.

This tender scenario of an Amish man waiting on his wife is very different from the image I once would have expected. And yet . . . the next day, after talking at length with Mary about how she and John divide up chores, I was reminded that I will never entirely figure out my Amish friends.

Mary and I and two of her girls went to the Amish goat auction in Mt. Hope, because she thought it would be interesting to me, and because little Susan was interested in getting a goat as a pet. Mary wanted to see what prices the goats were going for. As we walked through the barns, Susan saw an adorable miniature goat for sale, and we all fell in love with it. When the auction started, I leaned over and asked Mary if she was going to bid on it.

"No." Mary shook her head. "I'll have our eldest son take care of getting her a goat at next week's auction."

"Why?" I asked.

She looked at me as though surprised I would even ask such a question. "Because buying goats at auction is a man's job."

"Working Moms"

"This is how Amish women shop."

—AMISH MOTHER OF NINE PURCHASING GROCERIES
AT A "BENT-AND-DENT" STORE

Even though an Amish man might be more willing to help with domestic chores and responsibilities than I had once thought, it is assumed in the Amish culture that a man will work and provide for his family. A man's value in the Amish culture is not determined by how much money he makes or any perceived prestige inherent in his job. For an Amish man, respect doesn't come from a particular career. Instead, value is put on simply whether or not a man is a hard and honest worker and does his best to provide for his family.

This modeling of a strong work ethic for the men, combined with the Amish women's frugality, gives Amish mothers the option to stay home and raise their children.

That doesn't mean that Amish women don't work for pay, however. Many of the Amish women I know create home businesses that provide a good income for their families. My friend Gloria struggled with a debilitating illness for many years. When she found a health product that worked for her, she began selling it from her home. Eventually, she was doing so well financially that her husband quit his carpentry job to help her. They are now raising their five children together on their small farm, living out the Amish dream of working together as a family.

Amish women are not forbidden to work, make money, or even create lucrative businesses, but overall it would be considered odd for a mother to deliberately "work out" (the term they use in the Amish community for having a job that takes them away from home) once she begins to have children. Amish women who never marry or have children feel free to work full-time at whatever job they wish. The restriction isn't about women holding down jobs. The concern is about a mother's job taking her away from her children.

It is obvious that there are Amish women with talents and desires that go beyond staying at home and raising children, but in the Amish mind-set, the needs of others are more important than those of the individual, and they believe the needs of children are best served in their own homes, under the watchful eyes of their own full-time mothers.

There are many advantages to this. Amish children have the security and stability of staying home with their mother during their most formative years. Mothers take the training and teaching of their children very seriously. In fact, most Amish women I know find a great deal of satisfaction in their work at home. They see their role as being absolutely essential to the continuance of their culture. It helps greatly that their role is deeply respected within the Amish community.

Name any high-level position a woman might attain in the secular work world, and most Amish mothers would feel sorry for her that she has to "work out," and they will be puzzled that she would choose that position if it means leaving her children with someone else. A college professor, for instance, were she to visit an Amish home, would be treated with the same respect as the grandmother sitting in the rocking chair. Maybe a little less. Advanced degrees don't really compute in the Amish world.

One complaint I've often heard among Englisch mothers who have chosen to stay at home with their children is that they are often treated as "less-than" by others.

"When people ask me what I do," one stay-at-home Englisch mom of three fumed, "and I say that I'm raising my children, I get these pitying looks from people as though they want to pat me on the head and say 'Well, isn't that cute.'"

This attitude of being treated as "less-than" is pretty much incomprehensible to Amish moms, because they simply don't experience it within their culture. They know how important their role is, and they make no apologies for it. They take good care of their families, and when they can, they add to the family income with whatever extra skills and talents they possess.

Amish women frequently babysit for Englisch mothers who work outside their homes, but they secretly shake their head at the necessity for the Englisch moms to do so.

"The baby's father drinks and won't work," Naomi confided quietly, an Englisch baby in her arms as the mother pulled out of the driveway. "She *has* to work. Sometimes she cries when she leaves her baby with me and it hurts my heart."

I was recently reminded, when I was visiting with Lydia, how deeply rooted is this attitude against a mother working outside her home. She and her husband have a married child who is considering becoming part of the New New Order Church.

As usual, I was trying to understand the nuances between the various Amish sects—many of which make little sense to me. Lydia patiently explained that one of the differences people experience if they leave the Old Order for the New New Order is that they will be allowed to have electricity in the home.

This would be, she told me, a financial savings to them. She estimates that the battery packs and generators their family uses to provide limited electricity in their home cost more than being on the electric company's grid. She told me in her matter-of-fact way that her daughter would, of course, continue to use a horse and buggy even if they changed churches.

It was a surprise to me that her daughter's new church would allow them to bring electricity into their homes, but would not allow them to own cars.

"Frankly," I told her, "if I had to make that decision, I would choose to have a car over being on the electrical grid. It's just so much safer for one's children to be surrounded by metal and airbags than to be riding around in a buggy."

"Well," she said, "the way it has been explained to me is that in order to have ownership of a car, too many mothers have to work out."

The thing that is especially interesting about this philosophy is that it is almost equally applied to men. Fathers, on the whole, see being able to work from home—especially upon their own land—to be the ideal, but they will "work out" if that is the only way to provide for their family. At least, the men will "work out" up to a point, but if a job takes them too far away from their family, they simply won't consider it—even if the money is good.

When my eldest son took a contracting job in Afghanistan, the idea of him being so far away from his family seemed incomprehensible to my Amish friends—even when I explained that his earnings were going to be several times more than what he could make in the States. They were polite about it, but puzzled. Even the Amish men were puzzled. In their mind, for a man to leave his family and go to another country to earn money—even for a short time—was incomprehensible.

To understand their feelings about this, it is necessary to realize that while having a family or even being part of a family might seem optional to some Englisch men or women, it is pretty much the ideal to the Amish. From childhood on, nearly everything an Amish person does, or thinks about doing, is first seen through the filter of how it will affect the family. An Amish man, for instance, derives much of his feeling of manhood from the responsibilities of taking care of his family.

As I was talking to Lydia, I heard near-horror in her voice as she told me her thoughts about automobile ownership. The idea of a mother having to be away from her children in order to have money to afford a car was something worthy of lowering one's voice and speaking about in hushed tones.

I know Lydia's married child, and I don't think money is especially tight for them. I seriously doubt that purchasing a used car would put them into such financial straits that the mother would have to leave her children behind and go to work—but it emphasized to me the value that Amish women place on being able to stay home with their children.

As we talked, I looked around at her comfortable, roomy kitchen. Like so many Amish women, she, too, is a baker of bread, and there were several pans of it rising on the kitchen counter behind her. She, too, is a homeschooler and was flanked by her two youngest boys, rosy-cheeked and smiling, who were obviously pleased that I'd dropped in and interrupted their schoolwork.

Even though she was concerned about the possibilities of her daughter becoming part of a different church, I compared the peace that I felt in her and other Amish women's homes with the harried, rushed schedule I lived when my children were small, back when I was always holding down some part-time job. Once again, I wondered if perhaps the Amish aren't getting something right after all.

The work I did seemed necessary at the time. Nights on the weekend shift as a clerk in an emergency room while my husband finished his undergraduate degree. Full-time secretarial work in a nearby courthouse in order to help put him through graduate school. I spent time as a teacher's aide at my sons' school, which put me in closer proximity to my children, but it paid little. I worked part-time as a court reporter in Detroit, which paid well, but I grieved every day I had to be away from my sons.

When I was raising my boys, it seemed like I was always sleep-deprived, behind in my housework, and tired. I got through those years the best I could, hoping I was doing at least a tolerable job of raising my children. Like so many mothers, I simply did the best I could at the time and hoped things would turn out okay.

I have had a lot of conversations with Englisch friends through the years about the challenges of raising children while holding down jobs. Some mothers love their outside work and wouldn't have it any other way. They find the best day care option they can and make many contributions to society through their work.

Our church is blessed with several moms who love their jobs, are good at them, and feel that they are fulfilling God's will for their lives in using their skills and education to give to others. On the other hand, we have several who would quit their jobs and stay home with their kids in a heartbeat if they could.

I understand the decision many women make who choose to work outside their home because they have a skill that the world needs, or who are so gregarious that they derive energy from being around lots of other adults. What breaks my heart are those who desperately wish they *could* be more intimately involved with their children's daily lives, but—because of debt, a troubled marriage, or no marriage at all—do not have that option.

Having husbands with strong work ethics, combined with Amish women's frugality and a nearly nonexistent divorce rate, does create a situation in which Amish moms at least have that option.

"What if an Amish man refuses to get a job?" I ask Paul. "Or mistreats or neglects his wife and children?"

"It happens," Paul says. "Not often, but it happens. The men of the church will usually get involved under those circumstances and show him the error of his ways."

"How?"

"He'll be warned and eventually shunned if his behavior doesn't change," Paul explains. "It doesn't often get to that point. Most Amish men know what's expected of them as husbands and fathers when they marry, and they just go ahead and do it. It's what they know."

Regardless of how one feels about mothers of young children working outside their home, the fact remains, on the whole, that Amish women get to choose the option of staying home more often than Englisch mothers because of the work ethic and financial responsibility both sexes are taught from childhood.

I think we can learn much from a culture that makes it possible to have that choice, and the lesson has been brought home to me lately in a very personal way. My daughter-in-law is a smart girl who graduated from college with honors. She has spent the past few years working as an auditor for an accounting firm. When she became pregnant, the idea of staying home with her baby was a little scary to her because she'd had a job of some kind since she was about eight years old and took on a paper route. She wondered if she would miss going into work every day.

Then she had little Clara Grace.

"How could I leave her?" my daughter-in-law said to me with tears in her eyes as we discussed how grateful she was that she could stay home with her eight-week-old baby instead of having to go back to work. "How could I let someone else take care of my baby—or even worse—have to leave her with someone who might just lay her in a crib somewhere and ignore her?"

Fortunately for our daughter-in-law, she and my son have made some extremely frugal choices for a young couple. They worked at paying off school bills before she got pregnant. They live in a tiny log cabin where there is little space, but the rent is extremely low. In doing so, they have earned the option for her to enjoy nurturing Clara Grace as long as she wants, and I am grateful.

I have learned from painful experience that a discussion between Englisch women about whether or not to work outside the home can get heated very quickly. What a lot of people forget is that such a discussion is actually a fairly new phenomenon. Until the industrial age began, home was where you worked. To be at work *was* to be at home.

People made their living by engaging in various cottage industries, keeping small shops, and running family farms. The model for the common person was actually quite close to what I see among my Amish friends today.

On many back roads where there are Amish settlements, there

are little handmade signs at the end of driveways. These signs advertise things like fresh eggs and produce, birdhouses, honey, baskets, shoe repair, baked goods, and quilts. If you stop in, you'll often discover a small store in a corner of an Amish living room or basement that some woman runs while also tending children. This works well for them, and may, indeed, add to the contentment and happiness of their families.

Anyone who tries to use the Bible, however, as an argument that women should not work outside the home—as I have heard many times in my years in church—is skating on thin ice and has never taken a good look at Proverbs 31, which is devoted to describing the ideal woman.

In Proverbs 31, the ideal woman goes to look at a field and chooses to buy it. She plants a vineyard on it with her own hands. (She's a farmer.) She makes things at home and sells them. (She runs her own business.) Using her own money and skill, she makes certain her family is warm and well fed. (Her business sense and productivity provide enough to give her family an abundance of resources.) Her hard work helps her have enough to share with the poor. Proverbs 31 says that she even provides well for her maidservants, which means she had help with child care and housework.

This in-house help gave her the freedom to go scout out those fields, plant those vineyards, deal with merchants, and run a business. Although she is described as a woman who was devoted to her family, it is obvious that she didn't spend all day, every day at home.

It is fascinating to me that this biblical example of a mother as a strong, hardworking businesswoman was written approximately three thousand years ago.

Does this mean that every woman has to run out and get a job in order to be living in accordance with God's will? Of course not. Titus 2:5 admonishes the older women to teach the younger women to be "keepers at home" (KJV) or "to be busy at home" (NIV). I'm no Bible scholar, but it seems to me that the focus in both scriptures is simply that a woman should do what she can to take good care of her family.

Interestingly, the very technology the Amish avoid is now making it possible for many Englisch households to come closer to the Amish ideal of a family working and being together at home. There are now possibilities undreamed of only twenty years ago. Never has it been easier and more practical to create a home business with so little capital.

I believe that a mother's choices need to be respected. A mom who works away from home does not need to be second-guessed by those who stay home with their children 24/7. Nor should stay-at-home moms be treated with disrespect. There are many variables that factor into the choices families make. Sometimes a wife's income is high enough or her skill important enough that it makes more sense for the father to stay home with the kids.

And sometimes a babysitter might be a good alternative. In our church there is an amazing woman we often refer to as the Baby Whisperer. I've seen distraught infants calm down the instant they were placed in her arms. She loves caring for children and they love being with her. Our working mothers revere her.

Staying at home with one's children full-time might be the ideal, but after having worked as a court reporter for so many years, and with the divorce rate so high, it worries me a little when I see an Englisch mom utterly dependent on her husband's income. In a perfect world, a dad and mom would love each other, be faithful to each other, and nurture their children together. Sadly, that is not always the case.

Even when everyone is behaving responsibly, things can happen that put the burden of supporting the family on the shoulders of the mother. As one friend said who had to scramble to find a job when her husband became disabled, "I'm teaching my daughters to get a skill or an education they can fall back on. I tell them that it's great to be a stay-at-home mom until one's perfectly wonderful husband wrecks his back and can't work anymore."

From what I can see, there are no cut-and-dried answers about working mothers we can derive from the Amish models I've seen except one—children thrive best in environments where they feel safe and loved. Making that happen needs to be a parent's top priority.

Amish Parenting Tips
for the Non-Amish

- Spend time with your extended family. One of the biggest differences between the Amish and Englisch society is the interconnectedness of church and family members. Amish children grow up within a large group of people who care about them. To this end, give serious consideration to, and work toward, moving closer to at least one set of grandparents and/or other family members. Family—even flawed families with eccentric relatives—is important to a child's well-being. There is no law that says families have to live hundreds of miles apart. If moving is truly not feasible, try to intentionally create a family unit within your church, school, or community with people you trust and respect.

- Take family vacations. The Amish don't spend money on fancy things for their homes, but they do try to take some family vacations. As an Amish friend once said to me, "Even a bad family vacation is better than no family vacation at all." I agree. My husband and I and our boys had some lousy vacations. The one where mosquitoes nearly ate us alive. The one where we crammed all five of us in a tiny car filled with camping equipment and drove across Canada. The one where we accidentally stayed in a really creepy hotel. Our sons seem to think that even the bad vacations made good memories for them. They laughingly say that even though we suffered, we at least suffered together.

- Carefully evaluate activities, including all sports and all extracurricular activities, in regard to the effect they have not only on the individual but on the family. The parent who drives their child to the most ball games and ballet lessons doesn't necessarily win the prize for best parent.

- Teach your child how to grow something edible. Even if you live in a walk-up apartment, even if it involves nothing more than planting an herb in a tomato can, give your child the education of watching something grow.

- Learn how to cook. Whether you are male or female, if you can read, you can cook. The simpler the better. It doesn't have to be gourmet, but if your family has an addiction to junk food, start chipping away at it with real food. Nutrition affects not only a child's health but also his or her happiness.

· II ·

Community

Community

"I have never been lonely a day in my life."
—AMISH MOTHER

One evening, our Amish friends Mary and John invited my husband and me to a corn roast. John had recently received a huge, handmade, cast-iron grill made specifically for roasting food over a campfire, and there was a large field of sweet corn beside their backyard ready to harvest. John planned to toss some corn on the grill, along with some pork chops, and we would eat it all outside while enjoying the lovely late-summer weather. It was going to be just us, their family, and Joyanne and Clay. At least that was the original plan.

At the last moment, some out-of-town friends of theirs showed up as a surprise. Then nearby family members got wind that there was a corn roast going on and packed up and headed over on their tractor, pulling their children behind in a farm wagon.

My time in the area was going to be short, and we hadn't seen each other for a while, so Mary had invited me to come early to give the two of us some time to visit before everyone arrived.

I've discovered that a visit with Mary rarely involves just sitting around talking. Her hands are never idle for long. We were in her basement kitchen, chatting while finishing up the jelly she had been making. In addition to that, she was also turning out a couple of large pans of yeast rolls. There were dishes in the sink, children playing on the couch, and a little dog running around our feet.

Her basement has lots of windows, so we could easily look out and see what was going on in the yard. Several guests were already there, talking with John as he flipped pork chops onto the freestanding grill, which he'd hung on a tripod over the large fire pit.

Their eldest son had brought out all their folding chairs, plus some benches so that people could sit while they visited. Everyone appeared to be having a good time greeting each other, watching John cook, and getting caught up on one another's lives, but the more people showed up, the more nervous I got. As I hurriedly pulled jelly jars out of their hot-water bath and wiped them dry with a cloth, I was afraid there wouldn't be enough food, or enough seating, or enough of anything. It wasn't that I was worried for my own sake, or even the other guests' sake. I was nervous for Mary's sake. It was her party, and from what I could see, things were getting out of control.

"If this were my house and my cookout," I said as I craned my neck to look out the window at all the people arriving, "I would be freaking out right about now!"

"I tried freaking out once." Mary calmly placed the final dish in the drainer. "It didn't work out very good, so I never tried it again."

Mary's dry wit is always a delight, but as usual, there was wisdom behind her words. She did not go into hyper mode as I would have done. She didn't start yelling orders at her children while madly dashing around. Nor did she get the least bit angry at the fact that she was hosting more guests than she'd expected. She simply finished what needed to be completed in the kitchen, pulled a large casserole of potatoes out of the oven, and then the children helped us carry everything outside.

Of course, one thing you can depend upon with the Amish is that they seldom show up without food. Dish after dish was pulled from buggies and laid out on the table. Children ran into the house for serving spoons. The men plucked ears of sweet corn from the field next to the house, threw them straight onto the grill, and roasted them until the outer leaves were crisp.

After a silent prayer, we lined up and helped ourselves to the food, stripping the blackened husks off the corn and dipping the ears into a gallon jar of home-churned butter. Everyone had more than enough food, we sat on whatever was handy, ate off our laps, licked our fingers, and thoroughly enjoyed ourselves while I watched Mary sail calmly through the whole thing. Not only was she a good hostess, she appeared to be having a wonderful time.

Part of Mary's calm, I believe, was pure choice. Freaking out hadn't worked for her in the past, so she had decided not to do it again. And part of her calm was, I also believe, the determined lack of pride instilled in Amish individuals from childhood.

I've been in a lot of Amish homes, and I can't remember an Amish woman ever apologizing to me for the condition of her house. There might be some toys strewn about, green beans mounded on the table to be canned, and a menagerie of pets and children racing through the house—but there's never the apology so many of us Englisch women feel is required when guests show up. These women, unlike so many English women, don't expect their homes or themselves to be seen as perfect, and it wouldn't occur to them to apologize for not being so.

Some of Mary's calm was simply part of the Amish social culture. Next to God and their own children, the most important thing in their life is one another. Hospitality isn't just good intentions or nice-sounding words to the Amish. They see I Peter 4:8–9 as a scriptural command: "Above all, love each other deeply, because love covers over a multitude of sins. Offer hospitality to one another without grumbling." For my Amish friends, hospitality is a deliberate way of life. This impacts the children in a huge way.

"The one thing I miss about being raised Amish," an ex-Amish man told me, "is the incredible connectedness I always felt when I was growing up among them."

"Why did you leave?" I asked him.

"I was hungry for more education. I got a GED and then was accepted into a college."

"Was the college education worth it?"

He hesitated. Evaluating.

"I don't know," he said. "Some days I think so. Other days . . . well, sometimes it can get a bit lonely."

That loneliness seems to be an earmark of those who have left the Amish church. When former Amish people talk about what they miss most, it is never the rules and regulations, the worship services, the preaching, the lack of electricity, the horses and buggies, the clothes, or the hard work. Of all the things the ex-Amish may grieve, the loss that hits them hardest is the feeling of connectedness and close fellowship with their family and spiritual brothers and sisters.

Obviously they don't entirely regret their decision; after all, they could always go back. It would only take confessing that they were wrong, asking for forgiveness, and promising to obey the Ordnung, the rules each community member accepts. Frequently the reason they don't return is they've already married someone who is not Amish.

But sometimes it can get a bit lonely.

As far I can tell, as annoying as the rules and regulations of the Amish Ordnung can sometimes be, those few who do leave seldom entirely get over the feeling of disconnectedness they feel after they've left. I believe that, more than anything else, this is the reason most Amish people stay Amish. It is a culture that is intentionally designed to spend time together, help each other, and build a sense of purpose together. That has a profound impact on the way they raise their children.

Intentional Connectedness

"Sometimes our people gossip a little."
—AMISH GRANDMOTHER

One day as Joyanne and I are having lunch with some of our Amish friends, I ask a question that had been on my mind for a long time. I had been wondering if the tremendous interconnectedness of Amish people ever got on their nerves.

"Is there any downside to having so much contact with your Amish relatives and friends?" I ask. "Do any of you ever get tired of having such a close network of people in your life?"

"Sometimes a little." Laura is an earnest, intelligent woman in her late thirties. "But I have never been lonely a day in my life."

Joyanne and I glance at each other with envy. Both of us have known the loneliness of moving to a new city and trying to make friends. To hear someone say such a thing with such conviction is enviable.

"I think I was lonely once." Norma grins. "For about two hours. It was a couple of years ago."

Laura's younger sister, Beth, leans her face wearily into the palm of her hand and sighs dramatically. "I *wish* I could be lonely sometimes!"

At that, all the Amish women dissolve into belly-laughter.

I have seen these women working in each other's homes. Each one is as familiar with one another's kitchens as they are their own. There are reasons for this. They've helped deep clean each other's houses for church. They've eaten hundreds of meals together and then washed up the dishes and put away food. They've helped prepare for countless weddings and funerals together. There is a bond and a mutual understanding between them that feels . . . unbreakable.

One thing I know about relationships is that true friendships take time. There are no shortcuts to investing the time necessary to build relationships. These women, in spite of caring for houses filled with children, cooking large meals, caring for livestock and gardens, and sewing most of their family's clothing, appear to have the luxury of that kind of time.

There are many factors involved with this. Having no internet and no television helps free up a lot of time. Husbands who work hard to provide for the family help the women have more time to spend together. Mainly, however, these women intentionally and often make plans to get together—even if it is simply to take turns helping paint one another's living rooms.

As a young mother, I once talked with an older minister's wife who had raised four remarkable children.

"How did you do it?" I asked her. "How did you raise such wonderful kids?"

"One thing we did was have lots of good people in our house," she said. "Hospitality is really important to children."

"In what way?" I asked. "I can't see how having people over can make that much of an impact."

"Those who visit in your home can help validate all the things you are trying to teach your children. It isn't always easy, it isn't always cheap, and it is rarely convenient, but having people in your home is worth it. The presence of good people in your life can have an enormously positive impact on your children."

Those words have echoed in my mind for the past thirty years or so, and it is almost always in the back of my mind when I'm cooking for company.

When our boys were growing up, we had a great many good people in our lives and in our home, and it did make a difference. Our friends became our sons' friends and helped us watch after and nurture them. Even though my husband and I were living in an area where we had no family, we deliberately *created* a family with people who shared our values and morals.

In our overworked society, there is a temptation to isolate oneself and one's family and not bother with the effort of hospitality, but the Amish believe, as I do, that one's children will be shortchanged by it. I am forever grateful to the good people who were part of our lives as we were raising our sons. It made a difference in the kind of men they became.

The Amish obsession with connectedness does not stop with church services and face-to-face hospitality. Anyone who picks up a copy of *The Budget* while in the Holmes County area will be struck with how different it is from most other newspapers. *The Budget* is a weekly newspaper that has been serving the Amish/ Mennonite culture for nearly 125 years. It covers some local news, but the bulk of the newspaper is made up of homey letters written and sent in by "scribes" from all over. Both Amish and Mennonite churches are represented in *The Budget*, and every missive reads like a comforting letter from home, even if you don't know the people involved.

"Aaron got his new purple martin birdhouses built over the winter, so we're all ready for spring now," is the kind of thing a scribe might write. "We're hoping they'll come and nest and eat plenty of mosquitoes so we can do a lot of porch sitting this summer." Or a happy grandfather might write, "Our oldest son from the Oak Hill settlement came by last week. He took the old cradle we had stored in the barn back home with him. Looks like God is going to bless us with a new grandchild in a few months."

I've been to a handful of the settlements from which the scribes are writing and I know some of the people mentioned. I read about a fire in the lumber mill owned by my Old Order friends in Michigan and rejoiced that they were able to put the fire out and rebuild. An auto and buggy accident near Beaver? Oh, how heartbreaking. The Yoders finally got to have a vacation and visit their son in Sarasota, thanks to a neighbor willing to care for their dairy farm in Ohio.

For the modest subscription rate of $45 a year, reading these letters is an interesting way to cheer oneself up on a day when the world seems to be going crazy, and I am just an outsider. The Amish read *The Budget* from beginning to end as a way of keeping up with extended family members and friends.

In the absence of cell phones and texting, the Amish often stay in touch through letters. Amish girls are notable letter-writers, and some write to their Amish or Mennonite pen pals their entire lives. Letter-writing is a form of recreation for them, and pretty stationery is a favorite gift among school-age girls.

Paul Stutzman tells me there is also an Amish hotline, a number that some people use to keep up with Amish friends all over the United States. Those who access the Amish hotline speak to each other in Pennsylvania Dutch, of course, which is an effective way of keeping the hotline, well . . . Amish.

In other words, the Amish really, really like keeping up with one another and they put a lot of effort into doing so. All this connectedness gives the children a great feeling of security because their lives are so enmeshed with one another.

"Do you ever wish you had more privacy?" I asked Grace, a mother of nine.

"Why do you need privacy if you aren't doing anything wrong?" Grace answered.

The Amish have the philosophy that it takes both a family *and* a village to raise a child. The family is the first line of defense in a child's life, but if a parent falters in emotional or mental stability, has a troubled marriage, financial problems, illness, or dies, there is a dense community of Amish friends, neighbors, and relatives who can and will take over the care of the children.

The security of an Amish child is enviable. A huge percentage of them live in a household where there is both a father and mother. They are also wrapped in the security of a large, extended family, and beyond that, the church and church leadership are intimately involved in their lives.

I saw the effects of that security as I was having dinner with two Amish families one evening. There were around fourteen children present, in addition to their parents. While we got dinner on the table, the children were in another room. When dinner was served, they came out, filled their plates, and went back to the room in which they were playing. I didn't see any of them again unless they came back out to the kitchen to get more food.

In the meantime, the adults were having a nice, relaxing time together.

It took me a moment to figure out why this felt so odd, and I realized that what I'm used to, in general, are nervous, distracted, Englisch parents hovering over children who frequently don't get along well with one another and constantly interrupt with questions and squabbles.

These children were happily playing and laughing in the next room all evening. What I did *not* hear was any fighting, whining, or tattling. Not one child came out to complain about something to their parents. Nor did any adult go in to shush a child or to sort out an altercation of any sort. The children just . . . played.

I believe that kind of behavior comes from a deep well of contentment within the children, and that contentment comes from true security—the knowledge that all is right with their world and if it isn't, there are big people who love them and who will fix it.

Of course there are other factors—decent nutrition, lots of physical activity, lack of television and videos, regular church attendance, and parents who model nurturing relationships. But the fact that these children were so much a part of one another's lives, and were so used to being in close proximity, no doubt had more than a little something to do with their contentment and serenity as well.

Yet, the more I dug, the more I asked, the more I realized there's more to it than that. There is something deeply ingrained in Amish culture as a whole that makes these communities—and their children—act as they do, and I think it starts with the idea of *uffgevva*.

The Concept of *Uffgevva*

"Amish children are taught that they are not more important than others."
—AMISH TOUR GUIDE

I first heard the word *uffgevva* on a tour of the Behalt Amish & Mennonite Heritage Center in Berlin, Ohio. *Behalt* means "to remember," and in the center of the museum is a huge cyclorama depicting the history of the Mennonite and Amish cultures, starting with the crucifixion of Christ. *Behalt* is sometimes referred to as the Sistine Chapel of the Amish and Mennonites.

The Amish tour guide had just finished an excellent job of giving our small group an overview of the Amish and Mennonite heritages. As he finished, he asked if there were any questions. There weren't any from the rest of the group, so I asked mine, though it wasn't the sort of question he was expecting.

"You are in a position to see a lot of people come in here every week. In your opinion, what is the biggest difference between Amish and Englisch children?"

He seemed uncomfortable with the question. All of us in the tour were Englisch. He probably did not want to offend us, but he answered honestly. "Sometimes the behavior of Amish children is . . . better."

I pressed on. "In what way?"

"Well, for instance," he said, "my daughter has gotten to the age that she babysits sometimes for an Englisch couple with two children. Every time she comes home, she is astonished that the Englisch children will not do as she asks. Allowing deliberate disobedience in children is not our way. She is not used to it and does not understand it."

"I agree that Amish children are better behaved than Englisch children," I said, "but what I'm looking for is an answer to why. What are the parents doing differently? What is the key to all this obedience?"

He saw that I was serious, and he gave me an equally serious answer.

"Are you familiar with the word *uffgevva*?"

I shook my head. "No."

"Loosely translated, it means that you are less important than others. Amish children are taught from an early age, by example as well as words, that their needs and wants are important, but not *more* important than those of the family, the church, and the community. It is the exact opposite of individualism, which is what most American children are taught, and it is the exact opposite of what most American adults believe. It involves a surrendering of the will rather than emphasizing the importance of the person over the group. Ultimately, it makes a major difference in the way children behave."

I thanked him and pondered this philosophy long after we left. The idea is so alien to our culture that it felt uncomfortable even to me. One of the bedrock principles of American society is the worth and freedoms of the individual. The Bill of Rights, the Constitution, and many of the Amendments that have followed are about protecting the individual, the minority, the "little guy" from the coercive power of the state, the larger community. For most Americans, the need of the individual trumps the need of the group.

I don't believe there is anything wrong with that; in fact, generally I agree with the idea. But as I think about the application of it, I realize that the differences this philosophy makes in how we raise our children are profound, and probably go a long way toward explaining the differences I see between Amish and Englisch children.

When I mentioned my introduction to the concept of *uffgevva* to Paul Stutzman, he agreed that this is central to the Amish philosophy of life, and he gave me an example.

Until a few years ago, Paul managed a large restaurant in the Holmes County area. "I saw this played out over and over when I was working at the restaurant," he said. "A lot of Englisch children were so badly behaved that the entire meal was ruined because their parents were completely focused on placating a selfish child."

"I've seen that, too," I said. "In fact, I've had some uncomfortable meals while out with friends who were so absorbed in trying to satisfy their children's demands, it seemed hardly worth the expense and bother to have gone out with them."

"Exactly," Paul said. "I remember one family in particular that the staff and I dreaded seeing come through the door. Those children were so out of control that half the food ended up on the floor. The parents were miserable, the kids were unhappy, and we were not happy about having to clean up after them."

"They were not Amish?" I asked.

"Of course not. Amish children would never behave like that."

"And the Amish children?"

"In general, they were considerate of the rest of the family and acted like they enjoyed their meal," Paul said. "The differences in behavior the two cultures exhibited while dining out were remarkable."

For several decades now, the need to give children a good self-image has been drummed into parental consciousness, and we have responded in an interesting way. We have assumed that those children who are told that they are special and intelligent and gifted, who are showered with words of praise and approval and given trophies for their shelves and certificates of excellence for their walls will be happy and content and possessed of a healthy self-image.

Therefore, one could assume that Amish children who are taught that their wants and needs are *not* more important than others, children who are not constantly praised and who will never receive something as *hochmut* as a trophy, would struggle with poor self-image, depression, eating disorders, social maladjustment, feelings of inferiority, and a general lack of confidence.

That is not what has happened.

The Amish suicide rate is less than half the national average. Surveys have also shown that Amish teenagers have a healthier and more satisfied view of their bodies than Englisch teens. Anorexia and bulimia are virtually nonexistent in Amish culture. So are unemployment and homelessness. Obesity is much rarer among the Amish than the Englisch, and a survey of Amish women in Lancaster, Pennsylvania, concluded that on the whole, Amish women perceive themselves as happier, more content, and less stressed than those in a similar study of Englisch women.

And yet, self-image (or self-esteem) is not something the

Amish would ever think to worry about. Instead, their focus tends to be outward and more about being thoughtful and helpful toward others, especially within one's family, church, and immediate community.

Paul explains another Amish word to me, *gelassenheit*, which he says is ultimately at the center of the Amish acceptance of life. *Gelassenheit* is similar to *uffgevva* in that it is a giving up of will, but it holds within it the concept of *totally* giving up one's will to God. It is the idea of seeking and *accepting* His will in every aspect of life. An English phrase that partially sums it up is "Let it be."

The Amish often rely on this concept in order to shake bad things off and go on with their lives. It is easier to accept grief, for instance, when one believes that God has a bigger plan that He has put into place for our ultimate good.

I've already mentioned *hochmut*—the idea of haughtiness, arrogance, pride.

Avoiding *hochmut* absolutely permeates Amish culture. It is, for instance, *hochmut* to boast about one's biblical knowledge, or to praise a child's beauty or intelligence. Amish parents, for instance, would never put a sticker on the back of their buggy proclaiming to the world that their child was an honor student. To do so would be *hochmut*. It would embarrass them.

This ethic even affects Amish businesses. I was once talking to an Old Order Amish woman who ran a successful local mail-order business of tried-and-true herbal tinctures, which she made and bottled for various illnesses. Her encyclopedic knowledge of herbs and the exquisite care she gave to creating and bottling her products were impressive.

"I have several friends who would like to know about your

store," I enthused. "These have got to be the *best* herbal products I've ever come across."

She looked troubled and I wondered what I had said wrong.

"We Amish do not claim to have the *best* of anything," she gently instructed. "That would be *hochmut*. Pride is something we avoid. Instead, you are welcome to tell your friends that my products are . . . very good."

Amish children are awash in these three principles from the moment they are born: *hochmut*, *uffgevva*, and *gelassenheit*. I heard these three words mentioned frequently as I talked with Amish people about rearing children. They are a large part of what makes up the Amish culture and a key factor in why their children are such happy children.

Heritage

"Sometimes I feel like I don't know who I am."
—NON-AMISH MAN SEARCHING FOR HIS ROOTS

Connectedness, intentionally surrounding themselves with like-minded community, and putting the needs of the group before their own are not the only things that the Amish do to help ground their children in their world. They are also intentional about helping them understand who they are and from where they come.

The idea of heritage, and how important it is, was brought home to me when I was recently talking to Dr. Richard Rheinbolt, who has been a pediatrician for more than forty years. He spent many of those years as a missionary overseas, as well as working in various areas of the United States. I was chatting about the process of writing this book and I asked him what he would suggest, from his expertise, as an important aspect of raising healthy and happy children. His answer surprised me.

"Knowing who they come from," he answered. "Too many of the children and the parents I see in my practice have no feeling of roots of any kind. They don't know who their ancestors were or what those ancestors stood for. It helps give a person a feeling of stability to know to whom you belong."

I'd never really thought about it like that, but I could see what he was getting at.

My husband and I have a friend who was raised in a home he refers to as the "house of horrors" because of the abuses that took place there. The counselor he was seeing had a reputation for being especially successful with patients who had endured abuse. One of the assignments the counselor gave our friend was to do an in-depth study of his family tree.

It didn't make sense to me at the time—genealogical research used to address emotional problems—but it did end up helping our friend. It led him to travel even to other states for interviews with elderly family members he had never met. The revelations he received helped him better understand what was behind his father's abuses. Information about his grandparents and great-grandparents from both sides of his family helped with his healing. Eventually he ended up choosing the same profession as his maternal grandfather, a country preacher and a man of kindness and integrity our friend had never known but came to admire.

Dr. Rheinbolt's comment about the need for roots brought back a precious memory of my beloved great-uncle who took the time one evening when I was about ten years old to sit me down at his kitchen table, place a glass of milk and a plate of cookies in front of me, and proceed to tell me about "our people." While my mother visited with my great-aunt in the living room, he went back more than a hundred years, telling me stories of the good in which members of our family had been involved. His words have echoed in my mind for many decades.

"You come," my uncle told me while I munched cookies, "from a people who choose to serve the Lord."

My father, on the other hand, had little patience with family trees. When I asked him about my heritage from *his* side of the family, he told me that if I shook his family tree too hard, all that would fall out would be bandits and horse thieves.

I was unfazed by the idea of coming from horse thieves on one side and preachers on the other. The important thing was that I knew who I was, and from whom I came—and that was all that mattered.

What that experience taught me underscores the point that Dr. Rheinbolt was making. A sense of identity is one of the greatest gifts one can give a child. We are defined, to a great extent, by whom we love and by those who love us.

When my boys were very small and had some childhood hurt, I remember sometimes rocking them in my arms and comforting them by reciting a litany of the people who loved them. "It's okay. Mommy loves you, Daddy loves you, Aunt Sharon loves you, Grandma Ruth loves you . . ." And on and on until I'd named practically everyone we knew—by which time the child had usually stopped crying, and had begun to prompt me to mention the name of someone I might have forgotten.

One of the great emotional strengths Amish people have to rely on is that they don't have to piece together their family trees. They know exactly who they are, from whom they came, and to whom they are connected. You can hear it in the way they identify one another. There aren't a lot of unique names among the Amish. It is very unusual to choose, for instance, what they would consider a "fancy" name.

Therefore a community might have a plethora of Martha Yoders. If she was married to, say, Jacob Yoder, she would be referred to as Jacob's Martha. Or shortened to simply Jacob-Martha. A man might be referred to as Martha's Jacob, or by his father's name, as in Abraham's Jacob. In some cases, the grandfather's name might be thrown in as well: Henry's Abraham's Jacob. Everyone knows to whom everyone else belongs, and that knowledge goes back, in most cases, several generations.

Since present-day Amish came from about two hundred original families who migrated to the United States, when a child is being taught about the Anabaptist martyrs, he knows he is being taught about his own flesh and blood, ancestors who were willing to die for their faith. When a child is singing from the *Ausbund*, the traditional Amish songbook, in many cases he is singing songs penned by his own martyred many-times-great-grandfather.

If there is one thing Amish children know, it is who they are, from whom they come, and the principles for which their people have stood for hundreds of years.

This is potent stuff to a child.

Roots, to the Amish, however, have little to do with geographical locations. One thing that surprised me about the Amish is that they move around an astonishing amount for what tends to be an agrarian group. However, they don't move as individual families but in groups. That makes it possible for them always to have someone with whom they can establish a church. It is hard to be Amish all by oneself, so old people often move with young people. Grandmothers and grandfathers are brought along with the rest of the tribe, and the old homestead might be sold and a better one purchased. They have a strong sense of this world being temporary, and they value preserving relationships over clinging to a geographical location.

Sometimes pulling up stakes and moving is simply a financial choice. In Holmes County, Ohio, land prices have soared, making it possible for a family to sell one farm and purchase a much larger one in a less expensive part of the country. Sometimes an Amish family will move because they are unhappy with a minister or bishop, and rather than cause trouble within their church, they will move to a place where the bishop is less strict or, in some cases, more strict. Sometimes an Amish family moves because the parent church has grown to the point that they need to split and plant a church somewhere else. Since Amish churches try not to grow beyond approximately two hundred people, and since they are doubling in size about every twenty years, creating new settlements has become a priority.

This happened recently to the children of my friends Grace and Henry, who were simultaneously heartbroken and pleased when their son and his family were chosen by their church's lot to be part of one such move. But making the move was not a personal choice for them; it was a matter of obedience to what they believed was God's will and for the good of the community.

It meant the son and his family sold their house and a profitable business and moved far enough away that Grace and Henry must hire an Englisch driver if they want to visit their grandchildren. Still, they are happy that their son is faithful enough to the precepts of their Old Order Church to obey the prayerful decisions made by their church's leaders. Of course, as they were Amish, nothing about this move was done quickly. There were months of preparation before the mission group left the home church to establish the new one. But that didn't make it any easier for them to leave and start over.

The thing that fascinated me when Grace and Henry told me

about it was that there was never any talk about their son and his family not going. To disobey the call to create a new church and a new stronghold for another settlement of Amish people did not seem to be an option to them. The family would not have been punished for not going, but there would have been disappointment on the part of the church, and someone else would have had to take their place.

Yet again, because of *uffgevva*, others' needs were considered more important than their own, and with *gelassenheit*, total obedience to and acceptance of God's will, the decision to move was made.

How did this affect the children? It is early days yet, but watching their father and mother prayerfully make the decision to obey what they considered God's will undoubtably has reinforced the teaching that God's will was more important than the family business, their home, or their own desire to be within walking distance of their grandparents. It also created a situation in which the children and their parents would need to rely more upon the church members with whom they moved than on their own extended family of uncles, grandparents, and cousins.

The Amish heritage teaches their children that security comes only from within the confines of obedience—obedience to the family, obedience to the church, and ultimately, obedience to God. Not every Amish child grows up and remains Amish, but it is not for lack of knowing who they are and from whom they come. Even when they choose to leave, Amish people are so grounded in the principles and traditions of their faith that they carry that identity within themselves forever, and it gives them a framework within which they continue to live.

The Blessing of
a Second Language

"She has no English words . . . yet."

—AMISH MOTHER, SPEAKING OF HER PRESCHOOL DAUGHTER

One element of the shared heritage that unites the Amish is that they all speak a language unique to their culture. Most people refer to the common language of the Amish as Pennsylvania Dutch. Some of my Amish friends refer to it simply as "German," although it isn't quite the language spoken by today's Germans.

Pennsylvania Dutch actually differs somewhat from location to location. Someone who grew up in the Lancaster, Pennsylvania, settlement of Amish will speak it a little differently than Amish who grew up in the Holmes County, Ohio, area, but it is essentially the same throughout Amish settlements.

Pennsylvania Dutch is an Amish child's primary language until starting school. It is the language with which an Amish baby is surrounded while still in the womb. It is the language that a baby eventually learns to babble in, and it continues to be the primary language of the child until he or she reaches six years of age and starts school. At that time, the children begin to learn English if they have not already begun picking it up.

Mary's littlest girl, Susan, was fluent in both Pennsylvania Dutch and English by the time she was five, but that is unusual. It happened because Mary had been babysitting an Englisch child on a regular basis. He and Susan played together every day. Did the Englisch child learn Pennsylvania Dutch? I asked. Mary shook her head and told me that he was not interested, although they tried hard to teach him.

Apart from stumbling through a couple of years of required Spanish in high school many years ago, I am a one-language person. This fact never bothered me until I started hanging out with my Amish friends. Hearing them slip back and forth between English and Pennsylvania Dutch with such fluidity is impressive. They sometimes forget that I'm there in the room with them and fall back into the language in which it is easiest for them to communicate. When my eyes start to glaze over, there is usually some kind Amish person in the room who will remind everyone else that they are being rude, and suddenly everyone will smoothly shift gears and start to speak English again.

I'm grateful for their kindness, but I do tend to feel like the slowest child in the classroom when an entire group of people has to deliberately speak a second language just so I can understand.

Paul Stutzman, having learned Pennsylvania Dutch as a child, is fluent. When my husband and I have lunch with him in Holmes County, it is interesting to watch him easily speak English with us and then switch to Pennsylvania Dutch whenever one of his Amish friends walks past and greets him. He seems to do it so easily, it appears to be an unconscious reaction.

I have never seen an Amish person exhibit any pride in the fact that they are fluent in two languages. It's just a fact of their lives, and because they learned as children, it came easily. The thing is, the Amish aren't just bilingual—they are effectively trilingual. Their third language is formal German, the language Martin Luther helped define when he translated the Bible into the common German being spoken in the 1500s. It is very different from Pennsylvania Dutch, but the Amish learn to understand, read, and speak it because it is the language in which their church services are conducted.

"What are the advantages of being taught Pennsylvania Dutch?" I asked Daniel, a young Amishman who is writing a book and who had called me to ask advice about a publishing offer he'd received.

I heard a chuckle from the other end of the phone. "Well, it certainly helps your brain stay nimble from all the switching back and forth."

"I can imagine," I said. "But what advantages are there for the children?"

"There's an intimacy to it," Daniel answered. "For instance, when I was a little boy and out among Englisch people with my mother, I could ask her a question without any fear of embarrassment."

"Embarrassment?"

"Yes, you know, little kid things like needing to use the bathroom. Or why is that person in a wheelchair? The chances were good that she was the only one there who understood what I was asking. It was like she and I had our own private language."

"Sometimes," I told him, "I've wondered if Amish mothers are chastising their children when I hear them use Pennsylvania Dutch in front of me."

"Oh yes. My mother definitely used it to let me know when I

was doing something I shouldn't." Daniel laughed. "Mom's voice would be all gentle, but her words would let me know that I'd better obey, and quick!"

"I *thought* that might be the case."

"Well, sometimes they are speaking Dutch because it is the only language the child knows, but it was definitely a blessing to me when I was little," Daniel said. "My mother could gently instruct me privately, in front of a crowd of non-Amish people, without humiliating me."

Later that evening, my daughter-in-law, who is from Canada and fluent in both French and English, brought our newborn granddaughter over for a visit and I repeated this conversation to her.

"A private language between me and my daughter?" she said. "I love the idea. I'll start speaking French to her right away."

I believe that children who live in this country do need to speak English. It is the language of our nation. But I also see great value when parents who have been blessed with a second language take the time to teach it to their children.

I realize this is not always easy to do. I remember friends we met while we were in seminary who were Japanese. We shared an old house that had been divided into apartments. This Japanese couple wanted their small son to learn the Japanese language, both spoken and written. He went to an American school in Kentucky and he wanted to fit in. The last thing he wanted to do was speak Japanese.

The parents were wise enough to insist. Now grown, he praises them for it. During the recession, when he lost his job, he was able to get another quickly with a car manufacturer, partially because he had an intimate knowledge of the Japanese tongue.

This early-learned first language might also be partially responsible for the quick problem-solving ability a manager at a large business in Holmes County cited when I asked him if hiring Amish people—with their eighth-grade educations—ever posed a problem when he tried to train them for certain tasks. He told me that the opposite was true. He said that Amish workers tended to be among the quickest, best problem solvers he'd ever trained. This was especially interesting to me because there have been studies that suggest that a heightened problem-solving ability is one of the many benefits of learning a second language at an early age.

An Amish mother pointed out to me also that one of the benefits of Amish children not learning English until they start school at age six is that it helps to insulate them from the Englisch world. If they cannot understand our speech, we cannot say things that will damage them. If an Englisch person tries to talk to an Amish child, it is usually only through the filter of the Amish child's parents who translate.

The Amish as a whole have less dementia in old age than non-Amish. It might be due to a better diet; it might be all the social interaction; but some doctors believe that the mental calisthenics the Amish go through in communicating regularly in three languages might be part of what helps keep their minds agile.

According to other studies, a second language gives children an advantage in math skills as well, which might help explain why some Amish people can run international, multimillion-dollar manufacturing companies with no business degree and only an eighth-grade education.

Perhaps more important than all this, however, is that having their own language has helped the Amish retain a certain level of intimacy within their culture. It is yet one other way in which they are "different" from the rest of the world. It is part of the identity of being Amish, just like driving buggies and not having electricity or telephones inside their homes.

While researching a historical novel I wrote about Native Americans, I spent time reading up on the residential schools to which some tribes were forced to send their children. One of the especially heartbreaking things was that the children were not allowed to speak their own native languages in these schools. Many children were beaten if they used anything but English. As adults, they spoke out about how hard it had been to lose the ability to speak their native tongues—how it had stripped them of their identity.

If there is one thing Amish children don't lack, it is a sense of identity. As a culture, they know exactly who they are and what they believe. Holding on to their native language while also knowing English might be one of the wisest things the Amish have chosen to do in order to keep their identity amid the challenges of working and living within the larger Englisch culture.

Taking Care of One Another

One of the outflows of the interconnectedness in Amish societies—and, no doubt, part of the reason the groups are designed to be so involved in each other's lives—is that Amish culture allows families to care for each other in times of need.

I got to witness this firsthand one day when I was watching my first book, *Love Finds You in Sugarcreek, Ohio*, being made into a movie. The production crew was filming a scene where a home burns down. A Mennonite farmhouse had been rented for the set. The Sugarcreek volunteer fire department was there, and the house had been "burned" by temporarily applying black paper all over one side of it. It was nearing ninety degrees outside, and the firefighters were sweltering in their heavy, protective uniforms.

There were close-ups and dialogue to be recorded between the fire chief and the hero. It was a tense scene, made more intense by the sight of the firefighters in the background putting out the final fire with hoses.

The owners of the house and I, along with the sound engineer, makeup artists, extras, lighting engineers, and the real-life fire chief, police chief, and mayor of Sugarcreek stood in the side yard near a seldom-used dirt and gravel road, carefully out of range of the cameras. The sound engineer was struggling to get microphones positioned just right, and we were all being careful to stay very, very quiet on the set. Everything was perfectly coordinated to finish this scene and perhaps even stay on schedule for the day . . . and then a buggy trotted past and the dialogue stopped.

We waited as the buggy, with several Amish children peeking out from the back, drove past, its metal tires crunching loudly on the gravel road.

After it was out of earshot, everything was reset, the call went out for "quiet on the set," the water hoses were turned on, and the firefighters began to put out the pretend flames again that would later be put in by special effects technicians. The dialogue between the hero and the fire chief resumed. Everyone was busy doing their jobs . . . and then another horse and buggy trotted past. This time it was an elderly Amish man and his wife. Filming stopped.

Some Amish folk pointedly stared straight ahead, ignoring us, but many openly gawked, trying to figure out what was going on. I thought how odd this must look to them—a familiar local house covered in black paper, and the local fire department in full battle gear, pretending to put out a nonexistent fire. A steady stream of buggies trotted down this backcountry road while Hollywood got put on hold. This went on and on and on, and it would have been funny if our production company's funds weren't being used up with each nonproductive minute.

Frustrated, the director turned to the Mennonite woman from whom we were renting the house and asked her why there was this influx of Amish buggies on a back road. Why the sudden onslaught of Amish sightseers?

They weren't sightseers, she calmly explained. A neighbor was experiencing some unusually heavy medical bills, so they were having a fund-raiser at the Amish school up the road to help with expenses. The Amish families were not, she explained to him, driving by to see the filming; they were simply helping out a neighbor. Most would bring food, as well as pay for the opportunity to eat it.

The movie people gave up, sat down, and watched a lesson on rural Amish communities unfold. The volunteer firefighters took off their helmets and turned off the hoses as we waited for the dozens of Amish buggies to finish passing by.

Eventually the road was quiet again, we successfully managed to finish the scene, the dialogue was taped, the sound equipment was packed up, and the fire truck went back to the station.

The Amish people who were traveling past the movie cameras couldn't have cared less about this movie we were making about their culture. They had never heard of the famous actors involved in it. They had no idea that the sound of their horse's hooves and metal buggy wheels were causing a problem. They were simply doing what they have always done—helping out a neighbor in need. This is typical of the Amish. They help each other. Their communities are designed that way. The Amish community cares for its members. There's a mutual aid fund and a crippled children's fund; there are bake sales and lunch stands to raise money for needy families. Auctions generate revenue to operate the parochial schools.

The world has heard of Amish barn raisings, when hundreds of Amish people gather to rebuild a barn that has burned or otherwise been destroyed. Woman often have quiltings or do canning together. When a farmer is sick or hurt, neighbors will pitch in and plow fields, do the milking, or make hay—whatever is needed.

An Amish community takes very seriously the Bible's admonition to take care of widows and orphans. Those in sad situations will be assisted and cared for. No one is left to flounder about completely alone.

I once asked Paul what happened when an Amish family fell on hard times.

"Then the church helps them," he explained simply. "Their neighbors help them. And you have the Amish Helping Fund. The last I heard, that particular fund has around a hundred million dollars in it."

"That much?" I was astonished. "Where does it all come from?"

"Donations."

"How does it work?"

"It's available for leaders to use for specific needs they know about in their own churches," Paul explained. "A young couple might be allowed to borrow enough money to build a house or a barn, and then pay it back at a reduced rate of interest, or maybe no interest at all depending on the circumstances, instead of having to take out a mortgage from a bank at a high interest rate.

"Amish leaders also negotiate medical costs. There are hospitals that, if the Amish are involved, will knock forty percent off the cost right off the top. They know that if the Amish are involved, they can depend on getting paid. The fund will help cover whatever the family can't."

As I process the things I've learned about the Amish, I realize that these are usually not wealthy people, but still, out of their surplus, they help others. In some cases, there is no surplus, but if there is a great need, they will somehow find a way to give.

With extremely rare exceptions, the Amish do not accept government aid of any kind. No food stamps, no welfare, no Medicaid. There is also no Social Security to help cushion old age, or disability benefits if they become disabled. They do not rely on Meals On Wheels to help the elderly. They use no government funding for their schools or government subsidies for housing. Interestingly, even in a bad economy, it is almost unheard of for an Amish person to be unemployed for long. It's also hard to imagine any Amish person ever being homeless.

"What are the chances of an Amish child going into foster care?" I asked a group of Amish mothers.

"Zero," one said, and they all nodded in agreement.

"There's always someone who is willing to take in and love children in the Amish church," my friend Laura said with conviction. "Always."

Her sister-in-law gently challenged that. "I did know of one situation where an Amish child was taken into foster care."

"How did that happen?" I asked.

"The child went to a local public school instead of an Amish school. Her mother, it turned out, was dealing with some mental illness and was neglecting the little girl. The Englisch school teacher called social services, who took her out of the home and placed her with an Englisch foster care family."

"How did that work out?"

"The child cried and cried. It was so strange and frightening for her to be living in an Englisch home. She was so upset that the social worker took her out and found a nice Amish family for her to stay with until the mother could get some help. The child was much happier once she was in an Amish home."

"In other words, it is extremely rare for Amish children to end up in foster care," I concluded.

"That is the only case I've ever known," she said.

The Amish do not simply take care of their own. They are known for extending a helping hand to friends and neighbors who don't share their faith as well. I spoke with Beverly Keller, an editor of *The Budget.* Although the newspaper is for the Amish, Bev is not Amish herself, but she grew up next door to an Amish community.

"My father was a farmer," Beverly told me. "He was a good neighbor to the Amish farmers who lived around us. I'll never forget the day he died. . . ." Her voice choked up at this point and it took a few seconds for her to regain her composure. "The ambulance had not even left the yard when I looked up and saw our Amish neighbors standing there respectfully, lining the perimeter of our yard—silent witnesses to our grief."

"That's all they did?" I asked. "Just stood there?"

"Oh no," Beverly said. "Not at all. Soon after that, the food began to arrive. So much food! They did not intrude on our sorrow at all. They just quietly took care of us."

Joyanne Ham recounted a similar story. "We had not been in this area long. We knew almost no one. We hadn't even found a church yet. It was all we could do to try to get our bed-and-breakfast up and running. Then, suddenly, my father died. We brought his body here, expecting to have a very small funeral. We don't have a lot of family . . . or at least I didn't think we had a lot of family until our Amish friends began to show up. I could hardly believe they came. They seemed to know how badly I needed them. Their love and kindness was a healing thing. Those people really believe in Romans 12:15: 'Rejoice with those who rejoice; mourn with those who mourn.'"

"Did the children come, too?" I asked.

"Oh yes. The children were there, too," she said. "That's one thing you can count on with the Amish: the children are always there."

Less Focus on Formal Education, More on Lifelong Learning

"Having an eighth-grade education doesn't mean you have to stop learning."
—AMISH SCHOOLTEACHER

One of the distinctive aspects of Amish communities, and one of the more controversial for the outside world, is the way they school their children. As I dug into the reasons for Amish children's behavior, school came up again and again. I knew, from conversations with my Amish friends, that formal education for the Amish ends in eighth grade, and at first it struck me as strange. It's certainly not what I'm used to. Like most Englisch parents, I have always taken a culture of achievement for granted. The idea that it is a good thing to insist that a child graduate from high school, go on to college, and hopefully gain a graduate degree is something many of us never question. In fact, in some communities there is even intense pressure put on young children to perform well in school, as if the children's entire future depends on it. But, as I asked more questions, the reasons for the Amish model of schooling made more sense, and I began to see how the system is designed to intentionally foster the importance of family and community that allows Amish children to thrive.

One of the people who helped me make sense of it all was Albert. I met Albert, who was Old Order Amish, at the Gospel Bookstore in Berlin, Ohio. He was signing a book he had written about his specialized organic farming techniques and we struck up a conversation about it. As we talked, I discovered that he had organic meat for sale at a good price and decided to purchase some. The moment the book signing was over, my husband and I stuffed Albert's bicycle into the trunk of our car and we all drove to the house of one of Albert's relatives, where Albert rented a freezer and stored his meat.

Albert was an outgoing person, and as we drove, I found out that farming and selling books weren't his only sources of income. He had also been teaching for several years in one of the many one-room Amish schoolhouses that dot the landscape of Holmes County.

"So," I asked him, "what kind of training do you have to have in order to teach in an Amish school?"

"Eighth grade." His voice was matter-of-fact as he gazed out the window.

It was in the early days of my relationship with the Amish and I had not yet learned much about Amish schools or those who taught in them.

"You mean you teach up to the eighth grade?"

"No. I mean I have an eighth-grade education."

"That's *all*?"

"We find that is enough."

I was astonished. Many of my friends back home are teachers and they seemed to be taking near-constant college courses to keep their teaching certificates valid in our state. Most of my teacher friends either have graduate degrees or are in the process of getting one.

"Forgive my surprise, but I had heard that the Amish schools get their teachers from the Mennonites," I said. "The Mennonites are allowed to go to college, right?"

"Yes. Mennonites are allowed to go to college, but some of our Amish schools only allow Amish teachers, and I'm not Mennonite."

"So you've had no teacher training at all?"

"Nothing formal."

"But, how . . ."

"An eighth-grade education"—Albert's voice was gentle but firm—"does not mean that I ever stopped learning."

His answer stopped me cold. He is right, and I know he is right because I saw it in my own home growing up. My father was forced to quit school and go to work after he finished eighth grade, but his hunger for learning was never satisfied. He made his living as a sawyer, but read incessantly, memorized reams of poetry, and when I inherited his leather-bound volume of Shakespeare, it had been read to the point of falling apart. He did complicated math problems in his head and effectively tutored me in algebra when I was in high school. He taught himself to play the violin and in his seventies became a lover of opera.

So I have to agree with Albert that an eighth-grade education does not, indeed, mean that learning has to end. Still, few Englisch people would ever consider the possibility of jumping into a classroom as a teacher without at least a little training.

This is in direct contrast to a conversation I had recently with a young mother who lives in a large city. She had attended a parents' night at her two-and-a-half-year-old son's preschool where the teachers went on about how they were teaching pre-algebra skills to the toddlers. Soon after that, she saw an ad for someone who was searching for a math and reading tutor for her three-year-old. Hyperparenting excesses like these, she said, can make a parent wonder which is best—allowing a toddler to play and grow naturally, or putting them into contrived situations that hopefully create greater mental stimulation.

As she was talking, the image I got was of intense, nervous mothers hovering over unhappy toddlers who were trying to master long division.

Maybe it's just me, but when parenting starts to involve nail biting over the math skills of a child barely out of diapers, it might be a clue that for some people, raising a child has turned into a sort of competition.

We are a competitive society, so maybe it's important to continue to point out that there are no trophies handed out for super parenting. What we get out of having children should not be about competition. Instead, it should boil down to nurturing children well enough that they can grow into whole human beings.

Based on their cultural aversion to *hochmut*—pride—the Amish encourage cooperation and support for one another from an early age instead of fostering competition. It is one of the many reasons cited by Amish leaders for building and sustaining their parochial schools. Because of this, bullying, for instance, might take place in an Amish school, but it would be rare, and it would not be tolerated for long. If the teacher did not immediately step in, the chances are good that the other children would.

Albert gave me a short tutorial in the history of the Amish, and I learned that one-room parochial schools were not always the norm for them. For many years, their children were taught in public schools along with everyone else. In the fifties, everything changed.

Instead of supplying and supporting small, local schools, the federal government began building large, consolidated public schools and busing children to them. The Amish saw this as a threat. They wanted their children to attend local schools, where parents still had some say in the curriculum, and where the children would not be exposed to topics that go against Amish principles—like competition, secularism, and individualism.

Since the Amish leaders and parents felt like they had so little say over what was being taught, they began to build and fund their own schools and supply their own teachers to those schools.

During this time, dozens of Amish parents were arrested and imprisoned for refusing to send their children to the larger public schools. Eventually, the Amish sued, and the case was taken all the way to the Supreme Court. Even though the Amish rarely go to court, they did so for the sake of protecting their children. They won the right to maintain a community-based Amish education on May 15, 1972, on the grounds that a conventional formal education would interfere with the child's religious development. Legally the Amish could educate their children themselves and were no longer required to send their children to school past the eighth grade. This ruling was key in keeping their culture intact.

Our short drive did not give me enough time to ask Albert all the questions I had about Amish schools, so I later called Paul to interrogate him about this whole Amish schooling thing.

"So—exactly how does this work, Paul?" I asked. "Do the

Amish actually pay to build their own schools while still helping to pay for public schools?"

"They pay property taxes," he said, "which include school taxes."

"So they don't get any tax exemptions even though they don't send their kids to public schools?"

"No. A lot of people think they do, but the only tax the Amish are exempt from is Social Security, and that is because they don't draw from it."

"So you're telling me that the Amish people help pay for *our* schools and then turn around and pay for their own kids' schools straight out of their pocket?"

"Exactly."

"That doesn't seem to fit with Amish frugality. It can't be easy to pay teachers' salaries with no government help."

"The Amish are frugal, but they value their children's souls more than money," Paul said. "As long as they have some control over what their children are being taught and exposed to, they believe they have some control over their eternal destination. If the children don't go to high school or college, Amish parents feel that they are at less risk."

I mulled that over for a moment, thinking of more questions but not asking them, then pressed on, trying to understand why they do what they do. "But those children still have to make a living eventually, right? How do they do that without an education?"

"Amish are rarely unemployed. They have a good grasp of reading, writing, math, and geography by the time they leave school. Then between the ages of fourteen and eighteen they might be taught by older workers who will train them in various specialized skills—animal care, carpentry, masonry, plumbing, blacksmithing. You name it. It's kind of the Amish equivalent of vocational school."

I thought this was fascinating, and I continued to ask questions of pretty much anyone who would talk with me about the subject.

For instance, I stopped along the side of the road one day in Holmes County to admire some handmade baskets an Amish man and his son were selling from beneath a large tree. I could tell that they were Swartzentrubers, the most conservative of all Amish sects, because of the buggy parked behind them. The buggy was distinctive in that the orange reflective triangle required by law to be attached to all slow-moving vehicles was missing. These are supposed to be displayed on the back of every Amish buggy in Ohio, but you won't see them on buggies owned by members of the Swartzentruber sect. They view the vibrant triangle as decorative and have been known to go to jail rather than accept it into their plain lifestyle.

The young son was a good little salesman and encouraged me to purchase the largest, most expensive basket they had, which he pointed out was the perfect size to house several quilts. He also explained that it had a lid and could therefore serve as a side table. The price was surprisingly low, so I purchased it and several others I thought might be useful.

I paid the father, and as he helped carry the baskets to my car, we chatted about how many children he had and how they all were proficient at the family business of basket making. He was pleased that the children and his wife were doing so well at weaving that he could hardly keep up with making lids for all the baskets.

I had heard how ultraconservative the Swartzentrubers were,

and so I asked him about what his children did when they weren't weaving baskets. He said they helped take care of the farm animals, did chores around the farm, and went to school. I am always curious about what sort of books people read in their spare time and was especially curious about the books he allowed in his house. I had read that even children's Bible story books were forbidden by the Swartzentrubers.

"What kinds of books do you and your family like to read when you aren't weaving?" I asked.

"No cowboys and Indians," he answered. "No guns. No fairy tales."

I knew that "fairy tales" basically meant, in Swartzentruber terms, anything fictional. The novels I labored so hard over, both historical and Amish, would be deemed "fairy tales" by this man, and probably be dismissed as worthless.

Therefore I didn't mention to him that I was a writer. I already knew what his reaction to that would probably be. Silence. The Amish are good about following the adage that if you can't say something nice then don't say anything at all. Many statements or opinions are met with polite silence.

He told me that reading for pleasure, except for the German Bible, was not something he or his family often did. After all, they had baskets to weave and a living to make—but when I asked him what books his children studied in school, he could name every one and even told me which publisher produced them.

One of the sources of curriculum in his children's school, he informed me, were reprints of McGuffey Readers, the very same books my grandparents used in school more than a hundred years ago.

Whether their curriculum is at all appropriate in today's world

I don't know, but I'm deeply impressed that this man knew exactly what books his children were studying. I know that few Englisch parents would be able to recite the names and publishers of their own children's textbooks.

The Amish have real control over their children's curriculum and they take that task seriously. Ask any Amish parent which books their children are studying in school and that parent can probably tell you, partially because they are deeply involved, and partly because there is a good chance it is the very same textbook the parent studied in school. They have a deep sense of ownership of the school, because they, as a people, built and paid for it.

This is the way it works within the Amish culture. When a church district grows to the point of having enough children to merit a new school, the fathers of the children build it from donated monies and materials. Because they are Amish, there is never any lack of carpentry and masonry skills. Once the building is finished, a teacher is hired, again out of monies donated by the families of the children involved.

The salaries for teachers are not large. It is assumed that a male teacher will supplement his income in other ways. A female teacher is usually a very young woman who has not yet married and is still living at home with her family, although sometimes married women will teach if they have not yet had a child, or if all their children are school age. One of my Amish friends in southern Ohio shares the responsibility of teaching in a one-room school with her older teenage daughter. She and her daughter pack the four smaller children into their buggy every weekday morning and head off to school. She tells me she loves teaching, especially now that she has her daughter at her side.

Because they accept no government aid of any kind, their

schools do not have to accept any government mandates. Shirley, who is an Englisch friend and a devoted elementary school teacher, is envious.

"To teach, to have the freedom to just *teach* without the layers of regulation, supervision, and all the reports the government requires, would be so wonderful," she says with a sigh. "The amount of energy and time we teachers have to devote to testing and record keeping is mind-boggling. The moments of actual teaching in public education are much rarer than most of us would like to admit."

"I'm pretty sure that a large percentage of Amish children come to school after having had a good breakfast and ready to learn, too," I say. "I've also been told that discipline problems are rare."

"Are you absolutely certain they wouldn't hire a non-Amish school teacher?" Shirley's voice is wistful. "I'd be willing to wear a bonnet and a dress . . . if I could just *teach*."

There is one thing about an Amish education that brings about groans of envy in any school-age Englisch child I tell this to: Amish school teachers don't assign homework. Why? Because it interferes with the family. The Amish believe that the time involved in doing homework takes away from family life. As always, decisions are made based on the impact on the family. Always, always, the family is the priority.

The next time I saw Albert I asked him how he thinks Amish schoolchildren compare in knowledge to non-Amish schoolchildren.

"I can't answer that," he told me. "There are too many variables. Some Amish schools are better than others, just like some Englisch schools are better than others. We teach from different textbooks. There is no fair way to accurately compare. All I know is that our schools do a good job of preparing our children for the roles they will be filling in life. If a person wants to become a doctor, our schools would not be a good choice. If the same person wanted to be a farmer or carpenter or run a business, our schools would provide a solid foundation."

I knew that Paul didn't go to college, but I had never asked if he might have only an eighth-grade education.

"Did *you* go to high school?" I asked the next time we talked.

Paul laughed. "I did. But my parents were a little conflicted about it. After all, I could have been doing something useful instead, like hoeing corn."

"Were there any repercussions for you?"

"No. The first day of my ninth grade year came and I got ready and climbed onto the school bus. I knew I was going against my parents' wishes, but there wasn't a lot of discussion about it. I could be pretty hardheaded as a boy. They knew I wanted to go to school and they knew they would have to fight to keep me from it. My parents were kind people. I guess they figured it wasn't worth fighting about. Had they still been Amish instead of Mennonite, I would not have had that choice."

It's clear that he appreciates having been allowed to finish high school, while he also deeply respects the communities that do not allow children to choose. Not everyone feels the same way. I was recently involved in a discussion with an Englisch man who was relatively unfamiliar with the Amish and was quizzing me about their culture. He had no problem accepting the ideas of no electricity, riding in buggies, or even the restrictions on dress. The part he could not seem to get beyond was that they were not allowed to go to school past the eighth grade.

"That's just when their minds are developing," he said. "That's when their ability to reason and think really kicks in. How can they deny their children that right?"

He is not the only person who has brought that up. I have been asked repeatedly how Amish parents can take their children out of school just at the point when they are developing critical thinking skills.

I have also asked myself that question. Are Amish parents being cruel in denying their children a more advanced education? Are they robbing them of the chance to make different decisions about the course of their lives by sheltering them from the things that might lead them to question what they've been taught? What if there is an exceptional child with great potential to do things outside the realm of carpentry and farming? The idea of that child being denied an advanced education bothers me.

What I have seen within the Amish community is that sometimes children leave the Amish church specifically in order to get higher educations. I know of at least two medical doctors who chose that route. They still speak of their Amish upbringing with respect—but they hungered for more learning and chose to get it. One gentleman I've talked with was raised Amish, left the church, got a GED, was accepted into college, and graduated. He spoke of his Amish culture with nostalgia, but says his need for further education was too great to ignore. He also felt strongly that the profession he studied for, that of being a Bible translator, was God's will for his life. An Amish girl I knew who wanted to become a registered nurse simply became Mennonite in order to do so. Because she is still part of a conservative, Christian church, she is not shunned by her Amish church or her family.

In other words, it is not possible to be Amish and get a high school or college education, but, at least among the Old Order Amish, it is possible to become Mennonite and get both without being rejected for doing so. Advanced formal education isn't encouraged, and it isn't done often, but it is possible if a child wants it badly enough.

Most Amish teenagers that I've met, on the other hand, seem just fine with leaving school after the eighth grade—even eager. They are already competent workers and are anxious to get on with their lives and start earning a paycheck.

While many Englisch might be quick to criticize this schooling philosophy, it points to a fundamental difference in how education is viewed in the two cultures. An Englisch parent tends to view education as something that, for the most part, takes place in a schoolroom. An Amish parent views education as something that is taking place in nearly everything that happens in a child's life, and they take the role as teacher seriously.

I've noticed that nearly everything Amish parents do, they do with children around. This is not for lack of babysitters. There are always plenty of teenage girls willing to care for children. Instead, keeping children close and involving them in all facets of everyday life is an ongoing, deliberate attempt to teach necessary life skills and right behavior.

"When I go to help a neighbor," one Amish man said, "I always take at least one of my children with me, because they need to learn that it is important to help others."

Teaching a child to help a neighbor is admirable, but sometimes the Amish take this philosophy a little further than most Englisch parents would choose.

"Do you really take your children everywhere?" I asked Mary, thinking back to the wedding I attended where children were everywhere. "Is there any place you wouldn't take them?"

"Like where?" Mary asked.

"Would you take them with you to a funeral?"

"Of course." She seemed puzzled I would even ask such a question.

"Why?"

Considering the fatalistic mentality of the Amish, her answer shouldn't have surprised me, but it did.

"If anything were to happen to me or my husband, my children need to know what to expect, and how to conduct themselves. They need to learn," she said.

In the Englisch world, many parents tend to leave small children at home when they come to pay their respects to the dead. Children are shielded from death, and perhaps that is best—I don't know. My husband and I decided to leave our children home when they were small, and we went to the funeral without them. I didn't want to expose them to what I felt could be a macabre experience for a child. Many Englisch people also leave their children at home out of thoughtfulness to the grieving family. A misbehaving child in the grocery store is one thing; a child throwing a tantrum at a funeral is another.

In the Amish world, children are included, as with everything else, in the greater community as the people process their grief. According to Paul, there is no attempt to shield them from reality. Most have seen farm animals die and understand the reality of death from an early age.

I was once talking to a family doctor whose wife had been an intimate part of her grandmother's death from cancer. The grandmother had requested that her death would take place at her home. The extended family had flown or driven in to spend time with her, but the end had been extremely hard on everyone. Our doctor friend had supported the grandmother's desire to die at home, and afterward, I asked him if he would choose to do the same thing again or if he thought it had been too difficult for his wife and the rest of the family.

I knew his wife's emotional trauma had been great. I asked if a hospital would have been a more appropriate place.

"I've given that question a lot of thought," he said. "And I've decided that in spite of the pain, I would do the same thing again."

"Why?"

"Our society has deliberately distanced itself from both birth and death by allowing professionals like me to take care of everything remotely unpleasant. It might seem like a good thing at the time," he said, "but in doing so we have managed to plastic-wrap two major human experiences. Many fathers try to avoid anything to do with actual childbirth, and people try to pretend that death doesn't exist if they can't see it. In my opinion, that mind-set has created a very shallow society."

Because of the sheer numbers of people to whom they are connected and the habit of Amish parents taking their children with them practically everywhere, Amish children experience quite a lot of funerals. Thus they learn from an early age that life is finite. I think this creates a soberness in the Amish psyche at an early age. It is next to impossible to attend a funeral without thinking about eternity.

I am still uncertain whether it is better to remove children from the whole funeral experience, as my husband and I tried to do, or to take them along. Perhaps it depends, in part, on the emotional makeup of the individual child. What I do know is that Amish families face death like they face everything else—together. Amish children see their mothers taking food, washing dishes, and sitting up with the bereaved. They see fathers helping out with farm chores while the family heals. They learn kindness by observing and by helping as soon as they are old enough.

This is important not just because they learn to give of themselves when there is a tragedy, but also because they learn to have the assurance that the same will be done for their own family when the time comes. They are always, intentionally, being taught how to be a helpful part of their community.

I talked to Joyanne about this focus on lifelong learning, and she told me about one time when she saw Naomi handing a two-year-old a small grocery bag to carry into the house. "Here, let me get that," Joyanne said, thinking the child was too young for the task.

"No," Naomi said. "Please let him do it. He needs to learn to help."

The Amish man who runs the produce stand near my home nearly always brings one of his children with him. Sometimes the child he brings is too small to be of any real help, but he brings one of them anyway. Why? Selling produce is the family's livelihood. The child needs to learn.

Naomi's husband takes their eight-year-old son to the livestock auction even though they are not presently in need of any farm animals. Why?

"So the boy can learn," the father answers.

One of the biggest differences between Amish and Englisch cultures is that our children, on the whole, are taught that they must stay in school and get a college education if they want to achieve success and make a good living.

The Amish do the exact opposite. They encourage their children to opt out at around age fourteen, access an apprenticeship within their culture, and learn how to run a business or have a useful and marketable skill. Their sons and daughters are frequently self-supporting by the time most Englisch children are trying to fill out a college application.

Critical thinking and formal education are not necessarily tied together. Several employers with whom I spoke said that they prefer to hire and train Amish workers over non-Amish. When I inquired why, I was told that the Amish tended to have a better work ethic and a lot more common sense than those with more advanced educations.

I discussed this issue of education and common sense with a college professor I know who teaches at a state university.

"Academia often becomes a reality unto itself, which can cause some people to lose touch with practical things," the professor said. "Many of my colleagues and I are quite discouraged these days. Over the years, we've seen an erosion of integrity in the students we receive. Many of them have no real understanding that there are consequences for their actions or inactions. Most have a reluctance to accept personal responsibility for any problem those actions might create. Everything is always someone else's fault. I have also observed a decline in maturity and personal initiative. Kids are so passive about the classes they take. They seem to have no concept that there are requirements to pass a class. Many seem to be waiting for a college education to *happen* to them instead of requiring a great deal of work *from* them."

I hope it is simply the weight of a lifetime of teaching that is talking. My friend is nearing retirement and he's tired. I want to think there are many dedicated and motivated students, but one thing I do know is that on the whole, the Amish have a very different concept of the value of work and the value of education than the Englisch.

One difference in their concept is that the Englisch world tends to look for more significance in our jobs than the average Amish worker. In addition to a paycheck, we long for some validation in the form of prestige or identity, or at least some purpose. We talk openly of finding our "passion."

On the other hand, Amish people seldom equate their identity with their work. To the Amish, a job is a job. If it pays the bills, great. If there is a little left over to put into savings, wonderful. If the working conditions are safe, and the pay is enough to support a growing family, an Amish person is happy. This has far-reaching implications for how the Amish communities orient themselves toward putting the needs of the community above the desires of the self.

For instance, there are around forty different sects of Amish in the United States. The differences between them would seem petty to most outsiders. Why would anyone care if a member of his or her church drove a buggy with rubber tires or without? Or if the men of the church wore two suspenders, or one, or none—and yet these seemingly petty differences do separate the Amish from one another when it comes to the church district in which they will worship.

The Amish as a body are made up of autonomous church districts, with each church deciding and voting on their own Ordnung (their list of unifying rules). Some of these divisions have come from some extremely passionate differences, and yet, in a crisis, the unifying principles of the Amish still bring them together. A Swartzentruber Amish might not have anything to do with the Beachy Amish socially, but if there is a great need, they will ignore all differences and simply help one another.

The fact that they live in a culture that can put differences aside in times of need is yet another reason Amish children grow up with such a strong sense of community, a structure so tightly woven, dependable, and defended that it offers both children and adults a strong sense of security and safety.

Life for an Amish family revolves around community. From the tradition of multigenerational households to sharing of work to financial assistance, the community gives structure and support, and that has a lasting impact on the happiness of Amish children.

Amish Parenting Tips for the Non-Amish

- Hospitality is important. Don't be so *hochmut* (proud) that you can't have people over unless everything is perfect. Don't apologize for the condition of your home. It makes guests uncomfortable, and it can make your children feel ashamed. Most people care a whole lot more about being welcome than the condition of your home.

- Gently teach the concept of *uffgevva* to your children. Make sure they know that their needs are important, but not more important than the needs of others. Having children who aren't under the impression that meeting their demands is the purpose of your existence will not only make your job as a parent easier, it will take some of the pressure off your kids as well. Being the center of the universe is a hard job.

- Teach your children to be givers by becoming a giver yourself. Find a way for your child to help you help others. Even if it is nothing more than a jar of soup trotted next door to a sick neighbor—let your child help make and carry the soup.

- Find ways to incorporate teaching good principles into your child's daily life: the Amish try to follow Deuteronomy 6:7. To paraphrase, this scripture basically admonishes parents to teach their children godly principles while sitting in their homes, walking together, at night before bed, and in the morning after they get up—in other words, at every opportunity. This takes a conscious effort. For instance, instead of staying in a driving fog while taking children to various events, have a conversation with them, even if they are unresponsive. It isn't necessary to preach. Just tell them about your day, your childhood, your fears, your dreams. Let them know who you are, and what you believe in. This actually works. I was quite shocked when I started hearing my words coming out of my sons' mouths after they were grown. I would have sworn they had never listened to a word I said. When I commented on this, my middle son gave me a hug and said, "We heard a whole lot more than we ever let on, Mom."

- Build some practical hands-on skills into your child's life. Ancient Jewish tradition required its people to have a skill or trade even if they had a higher education. A good example from the Bible is the apostle Paul—who had studied at the feet of the great Rabbi Gamaliel the Elder and basically had the first-century equivalent of a PhD. Yet he also had a skill. He was a tent maker, which came in quite handy when he needed to support himself. A woman I know said that her grandmother was a tailor who taught her how to sew. The grandmother had told her that if she knew how to sew, she would never go hungry. Even though the woman had a professional life apart from sewing, she said that in the back of her mind there was always the comfort of knowing that if necessary, she could support herself with her sewing ability—just like her grandmother.

- Roots are important. If you don't know what yours are, find out. Give your child a sense of who his or her people are. There are many online programs to help you in your search. Make it a family project.

- If you are blessed with a second language, teach it to your child as early as possible. If you don't know a second language, it might be something you can learn together.

· III ·

Discipline

Discipline

"Our homes are not child-centered. They are God-centered."
—AMISH MINISTER

I knew an Englisch mother who did not believe in correcting her child . . . at all. She was a brilliant, well-educated, delightful woman, but she was of the opinion that rules and correction stymied a child's development. It was interesting to watch this philosophy play out in the child's behavior and the parents' struggle to raise him. He was a normal child with no inherent psychological problems that I could see; however, with no correction or guidance, he was the most poorly behaved child I'd ever known.

He wanted to play and have friends, but his behavior was so off-putting to other children that they did not want to be around him. He seemed to have no control over himself. I was present once when he went into a total meltdown and told his mother that everyone hated him. His mother comforted him by telling him that he was mistaken and that everyone loved him.

Later, I described the scene to a friend who was an experienced child counselor. The counselor said that children raised with no boundaries were usually miserable because they had no idea how to relate to others. She said a child raised without rules was like a car careening down the road with no guardrails. Everyone knew there would be a wreck; it was just a matter of time.

In a sociology class many years ago, the professor told us about a study done on children's basic need for rules. On a large, inner-city school playground, researchers tested the need for structure with small children. They let the children freely play on a playground that had no fence around it. The children instinctively clustered close to the teachers who were standing outside watching them. The children were careful not to go near the edges of the playground.

The sociologists then erected chain-link fences around the playground. The behavior of the children immediately changed. They spread out all over the playground and their play became more happy and free. It was apparent that with the fence in place, the worry was gone and the children could enjoy themselves. There were clear-cut boundaries.

Not having rules is most definitely not a problem for Amish children. If there is one thing they have, it is structure and routine. Assigned chores, family meals with prayer, and sometimes family devotionals in the evening bracket and define their day. Regular church services punctuate each month. Frequently there are chores assigned to each specific day of the week: Monday is wash day if the weather is fine, Tuesday ironing day, and so on, much as our great-grandmothers lived.

There are also unwritten rules about relating to other children. In a society as closely knit as the Amish, kind and thoughtful behavior is imperative. Children are taught to respect other children and siblings as well as their parents and teachers.

I can't help but compare that poor child's out-of-control behavior with what I've seen of Amish children playing together.
It is obvious that Amish children are taught rules and boundaries. They know that their needs and wants are not more important than the other children's. They automatically compromise
and also end up playing happily together because they have been
taught kindness and forgiveness from the cradle on. Astonish-
ingly, I've never seen an Amish child given a "time-out" or be told
to go to their room. What I have seen instead is cheerful obedience by the children. Over and over I have asked Amish parents
how they do it.

Once again, their answers surprised me.

More than Happy

"My dream for my children is that they grow up to be people of value."
—AMISH MINISTER

My husband and I were talking with some Amish fathers recently about the role of discipline and hard work in raising Amish children. My husband had a question for the men. "As fathers, what is your dream for your children?"

All three men took time to ponder this. As they thought this through, I rolled various possible answers around in my mind. How would most Englisch parents respond? Would they say they dream of happiness for their children? Good health? A good education? Maybe a great job?

When our friend Lester answered, it was none of these things. "My dream for my children is that they grow up to be people of value."

He did not add to that statement. That was his dream for his children. Period.

"And if I want my child to grow into a person of value," Lester said, "there must be consequences to my child's actions. Otherwise he will grow up wild and be of no use to himself or to others. I look at it this way: there are consequences because I love you. If I didn't love you, I would go about my business and not bother trying to discipline you."

The wording of this simple comment struck me as profound. He was explaining his dreams and desires for his children, and yet he spoke in terms of discipline and consequences.

So many of the Englisch parents I know would probably say that their greatest desire for their children is that they will grow up to be happy people. As I've interviewed my Amish friends, one thing has been made very clear to me: happiness is not their primary objective. Not for their children and not for themselves. Happiness is seen as a *by-product* that comes from treating others well.

Instead, they concentrate on helping their children grow into people of value—sons and daughters with integrity and compassion who know how to work and how to give. One of life's ironies is that children who grow up to become people of value also tend to end up being very happy people. On the other hand, children who have been placated, bribed, given no responsibility and too many possessions, who are not taught clear-cut values and rules or how to do a day's work . . . these children tend to become pretty miserable pretty quickly.

Parents who fall into the trap of constantly trying to keep their child "happy" (versus not giving in to everything the child wants) can make some very unhealthy decisions, not only for their child but for other children as well.

For example, my husband and I were recently in one social situation where a four-year-old got into the host's kitchen drawer and pulled out a screwdriver as several of us milled around helping get dinner ready. There were other children playing nearby as the four-year-old brandished the screwdriver.

"Your kid has a screwdriver," my husband pointed out to the other father.

The father turned to the child, said "Let me have that," and tried to take the screwdriver out of the little boy's hand. The minute he tugged on the tool, the child tightened his grip, screwed up his face, and started to cry. The father let go, and the child stopped crying.

This scenario was repeated a couple more times.

"I can't take it away from him," the father said, giving up.

"Why not?" my husband asked.

"Well . . . because he'll cry," the father said.

My exasperated husband, who feared the boy might skewer one of the other children with the sharp tool, plucked the screwdriver out of the child's hands, sat it out of reach on top of the refrigerator, and said, "Then let him cry."

The look of shock on the four-year-old's face matched his father's. The child plopped himself down in the middle of the kitchen floor and sent up a howl. The rest of us simply walked around him for a while. The father shrugged, then went off to watch a football game in the other room. Realizing he was being ignored, the child eventually stopped crying and went off to play with the other children.

Something that seemed so basic to us—preserving the safety of the other children, as well as the child's own safety—did not compute with this parent, who had evidently spent most of the past four years placating a child that he desperately wanted to keep . . . happy.

I can't imagine this same scenario playing out with an Amish parent and child. A child's possession of a certain toy, for instance, is not considered a necessity. The child's ability to wait patiently for the toy *is* considered a necessity.

In the famous "marshmallow" experiment performed by psychologist Walter Mischel, who was a professor at Stanford University in the late 1960s and early 1970s, a young child would be offered the choice between a small reward, such as a marshmallow to be eaten immediately, or two small rewards if he or she waited until the tester returned after an absence of about fifteen minutes.

Some children ate the marshmallow right away. Others covered their eyes, turned around in their seats, or used other techniques to help them not give in to the temptation of immediately eating the treat.

In follow-up studies many years later, the researchers found that the children who were able to wait longer for gratification tended to have higher SAT scores, higher educational attainments, and even a better body mass index (BMI) and other quality-of-life measures.

Most Amish parents would not be familiar with this experiment, but I doubt that they would be surprised by the outcome. Teaching a child the ability to wait is deliberately built into the Amish style of parenting.

For instance, here is a letter I received last fall from an Amish grandmother with whom I had discussed parenting a few weeks earlier.

> *I am just trying to clean up for fall and do some visiting. I like it that me and my sisters go on visits or go out to eat about every two weeks. We were up to my daughter's on Saturday to help clean and move her into their new house.*

I was going to tell you the last time I saw you that when I used to take the kids along to a store, I always warned them that if they were on their good behavior I would buy them something like gum or candy. They knew what Yes or No meant.

Esther's letter underscores what I've seen with my other Amish friends when we go shopping. Whereas an Englisch parent might purchase a toy or treat during a shopping trip with a child in order to keep that child content (or in some cases to keep the child from throwing a tantrum in the aisles), an Amish parent will purchase a treat or small toy only *because* the child had been quiet and content.

The difference is subtle but extremely telling.

The Englisch parent is basically *bribing* the child into good behavior, but the Amish parent is *rewarding* the child for self-discipline. Done consistently, this system pays great dividends. The quiet, obedient Amish child you might see in the grocery store is probably busily calculating how many more minutes of good behavior is expected before his or her mother or father buys them a treat. One thing an Amish child knows absolutely is that there will be no treat if pleading and whining are involved.

There's a good reason for an Amish parent to focus so much on discipline, beyond merely avoiding the annoyance of a demanding child. It also helps preserve their culture.

It is extremely rare for an Englisch person to convert to the Amish church. Since 1950, there reportedly have been only about seventy-five who have attempted it. Of those seventy-five, about half eventually returned to Englisch society.

One of the reasons well-intentioned people find it too hard to become Amish is that the Amish life takes enormous self-discipline, especially in the area of giving up self for the greater good. Amish parents don't love their children any less than Englisch parents, but they know that teaching a child how to discipline themselves enough to live an obedient and faithful life is necessary in order to keep a child within the faith.

A selfish, disobedient, rebellious child is not going to stay Amish for long—and parents know that.

I've seen some Englisch parents' love for their children, however, sometimes bordering a little too close to worship. If parents aren't careful, they can find themselves in the role of a supplicant to a small, demanding deity.

Amish families worship God and God alone, and that helps them keep their children centered and balanced. Amish children are loved and they are given plenty of attention, but they learn early on that they are not the center of the universe. It is a good reminder, indeed.

Teaching Respect

"Children don't become respectful by accident."
—AMISH MOTHER

Self-discipline is not the only reason Amish children behave so reliably well, though. It took a while for me to pin down what it is, but eventually, as I spent more time with my Amish friends, I began to notice something. Respect for others is also deliberately built into the fabric of their lives and stands as an example to the children.

For example, when an extended Amish family has a potluck, the grandfather and grandmother are always given precedence in the food line. A mother might, while setting out the meal, give a young child a small snack to tide the child over, but for the most part, children are taught to hold back from getting in line until the older people have been served.

I find this in direct contradiction to most Englisch potluck situations—even in church settings—where the children race and push ahead to be first in line, almost as though it is a game they must win. There have been times when I've worried that the more fragile, older people in our church might get knocked over because of the children's single-minded determination to get there first.

Older people's appetites are not usually as aggressive as small children's, and I see the older people holding back and allowing the children to go first—but there is a cost to pay. It is a subtle way of telling the children that the older people don't matter. It can give children the impression that their own needs and appetites come first and foremost.

Amish women tend to hold back and allow the men to go first in a food line as well. I had noticed this and mentioned it to Leah. Was this an example of sexist, subservient behavior?

Leah laughed at my concern and explained the reasoning behind it.

"My mother always taught us girls that the reason we should allow the men to eat first is because if there wasn't enough food prepared, it was our own fault!"

Naomi explained it to me in a different light. "My husband works hard outdoors and gets so very hungry. I have time to sample a bit of food while I'm cooking but he doesn't have that opportunity. My appetite simply isn't as great."

Holding back. Allowing men to go first. Allowing the older people to go first. These things are not questioned, except by Englisch guests. It is simply the way things are and always have been. It is also an example of the quiet thoughtfulness I have seen exhibited over and over in the Amish culture.

On the other hand, "men first" doesn't always apply. I've had Amish male hosts step back and motion for me to go in line before them. This, too, is a matter of traditional respect that has nothing to do with gender. I'm a guest, and guests are invited to go first. That's just how it is done.

Respect is also quietly shown in the way the Amish file into a residence or building where they are holding church services. The bishop—who is head of their church—will enter first. Then the ministers file in, usually in order of how long they have served.

Eventually the rest of the men come in, according to age. The teenage boys come in at the end. The women usually go in by a different door and sit separately on the other side. As with the men, the older women enter before the younger. Respect is modeled in a very visible and structured way.

I'm curious about other ways they incorporate respect for others into how they live and model behavior for their children, so I press my friends.

"In what areas do you see the Englisch lacking respect?" I ask at lunch one day. "Is there anything you've ever seen Englisch people do that made you wish you could give them a good talking-to?"

They ponder this a moment, and I wonder if they are holding back in order to spare my feelings.

"Yes," Mary finally speaks up. "There is one situation in which I've really had to hold my tongue."

I lean forward. "What is that?"

"It is the tone of voice in which I've heard Englisch women speak to their husbands." She shakes her head disapprovingly. "How can a mother expect her children to respect and obey their fathers if those mothers talk to their husbands with such disrespect?"

"It is not always Englisch wives who do that," her sister-in-law, Rebecca, points out. "I've heard it come out of the mouths of Amish wives a few times, too."

"But not as much," Mary says.

"No, not nearly as much," Rebecca concedes. "An Amish man

would not stand for it, but it is a real problem with Englisch women. I hear it all the time when I'm shopping. I wonder if they realize how ugly it makes them sound. They talk that way to their children, too. No wonder the children talk back so disrespectfully. That is the way they have been taught."

In Mary's home, there is laughing, joking, serious discussion of heavy issues, and open discussion of biblical issues . . . but each person's thoughts and comments are given consideration and weight.

I have never yet heard disrespect in an Amish parent's voice when they were talking to a child, even if the words hold a mild chastisement. On the other hand, just like my Amish friends, I have frequently cringed at the humiliating way Englisch parents speak to their children in public.

"You little wimp!" I remember an angry parent yelling at his small child who was reluctant to go into a wading pool that the parent had just purchased. "That's all you are. A wimp! Get into that water right now!" This from the mouth of an educated parent who I knew loved his child.

"My daddy is nothing but a big, lazy slob!" an eight-year-old girl informed me once while I was teaching a Sunday school class. "All he does is lay around watching TV all the time."

I could practically hear her mother's contemptuous tone in the little girl's voice and I thought that there had probably been an ugly altercation in that home recently. I knew the family and knew that the father worked hard at a miserable job in order to provide for his family. Lazy? Not really. But the child had the mother's contempt down cold. Even her stance—hands on hips, curled lip—was a mirror of what I imagined her mother doing when she threw those words at him in front of the children.

"You forgot to put the butter on the table again!" an Englisch teenage boy growled at his mother in front of me and the rest of our family. "You're always forgetting things. Why can't you remember to put butter on the table?"

"Oh! I'm sorry!" His mother, a sweet, harried woman, scurried into the kitchen and brought the butter dish.

She had cooked a marvelous meal for us, and had been rushing around trying to get dinner on the table with help from me and another guest. The boy had done nothing except shove himself up off the couch where he'd been watching television and plop himself down at the table, then surveyed the food set out in front of him.

His tone was dripping with such contempt I felt myself flush with embarrassment for the woman, and I wondered why her husband didn't jump up from the table, take the boy outside, and teach him to have a little more respect for his mother. Instead, the father acted completely oblivious and we all continued on with dinner as though nothing had happened.

My eldest son, who was about the same age as the teenager, commented on that little scene a few hours later.

"Dad would have come right over the table at me if I ever talked to you like that," he said.

"He wouldn't have to." His younger brother looked up from a comic book he was reading. "Mom would have beat him to it."

Both sons seemed strangely proud of the fact that they could not get by with the kind of disrespectful behavior they had just witnessed.

These are extreme examples, but there are less notable ones that are just as destructive. Comparing children to one another is also toxic and a great way to cause a child to give up on good behavior and start rebelling. A constantly dismissive tone or overused sarcasm can destroy a child. Impatience can become a habit, and an attitude of constant impatience with one's child or one's spouse can become a form of emotional abuse. I have watched it over and over. Speaking with respect about and to one another is one of the healthiest things parents can do. Not only do children learn to respect their parents from watching and hearing it, but oddly enough, they tend to have a little more respect for themselves.

Disrespect isn't always presented with a contemptuous tone. A jocular, happy tone can do just as much damage. Humor can be a great thing in a family, but not if it involves belittling one another. A mother can turn her husband into a hero in her children's eyes, or a buffoon—just with the words she chooses to use when she talks to or about him. A father can do the same thing to the mother. "Friendly fire" is a military term, used when personnel are accidentally killed or wounded in battle by fellow soldiers. A contemptuous tone or a misguided need to draw a cheap laugh can damage the very people we love just like those "friendly fire" bullets. It's wise to pay attention.

"John is a hard worker and a good provider," Mary tells me as we wash dishes together. "He has been a good husband to me and a loving father to our children. This has been a great blessing to our family."

Her children are nearby. With a couple of sentences, she has defined her husband in her children's eyes. These gentle words also give her children a sense of security and peace when they hear their mother speak them out loud. I can see it in their faces.

Another way the Amish demonstrate respect for one another is in what my husband has termed the Amish Pause.

There have been several studies of how often certain people are interrupted in social interactions. Sometimes gender plays a role—men tend to be interrupted less than women. Sometimes it is a matter of a relationship—spouses tend to interrupt one another more frequently. Sometimes it is simply the perception by which a person is viewed by others. An "important" person is interrupted less often than an "unimportant" person. For instance, a stay-at-home mom might be interrupted more often than an attorney, regardless of gender, the topic of conversation, or the stay-at-home mom's educational status. A doctor or college professor is less likely to be interrupted during a dinner party than someone with less education. Someone who is perceived as rich will probably not be interrupted as often as someone who is perceived as poor.

Over the years, I've quietly watched this play out in social settings again and again, and it is always interesting to observe. It is a totally unconscious and innocent social reaction, this automatic evaluation of someone else's level of importance by the conversational group's yardstick, but it is there.

Sometimes you can see someone who is frequently interrupted in a room of people eventually give up trying to be a part of things and grow silent. I've seen this happen especially with elderly women.

We are aggressive talkers in my family. We tumble about all over one another's words, because when we get together, we all have so much to say. It is often hard for any of us to get through an entire story without being interrupted several times. This applies to everyone in our family except for our youngest son, who was born quieter than the rest of us. He also developed a bad stuttering problem.

A speech therapist who knew our family was working to help our son overcome this problem. At one point, she suggested that it would help a lot if we could ever quit talking long enough to let him get a word in edgewise. She instructed us to pause in our conversation at the dinner table several times each evening so he could talk, and to remember to respect his words. We were not to interrupt him no matter how long it took for him to get his words out.

It took discipline on our part to remember to respect a six-year-old's words, but eventually he began to speak more easily. He's an adult now and no longer stutters, but when he and his brothers are together, I'll sometimes hear him threaten to start stuttering again if they don't shut up and listen to him.

Conversational interruptions are not a big problem in an Amish home. What I've seen during get-togethers with the Amish is that first of all, the conversation is much less hurried than in Englisch social situations. In an Amish group, each person's comment tends to be given more thought. I've often even noticed a respectful pause after someone has spoken, while everyone politely ponders and weighs what has just been said.

When I first began to spend time with the Amish, this slight hesitation in their speech seemed awkward to me and I felt like I needed to jump in and fill the silence. That was before I realized that it was an unconscious show of humility.

The first time I met Luke, for instance, the pleasant young Amish father listened politely to a question I asked him and then thought it over before answering. It was early in my relationship with the Amish and it seemed to me that he was pondering my question a lot longer than necessary. Uncomfortable with the silence, I jumped in and repeated it in what I considered simpler terms. Then I waited, once again, for the answer. The halting, question-pause-answer conversation went on for a bit and I came to the conclusion that Luke might not be the brightest bulb on the Christmas tree.

I've known Luke for several years now and have discovered that he is one smart cookie. He runs a profitable business and makes a good living for his family. The problem with our initial conversation was that I did not understand the Amish Pause.

Many Englisch people speak fast and answer quickly, even finishing each other's sentences to make the conversation move along, as though they are rushed for time, no matter what the situation is. Silence seems to be the enemy.

The Amish have no problem with silence. They tend to speak slowly and take time thinking things through before they speak. Words are carefully considered and then an answer or opinion is given. Like so much else the Amish do, it is a matter of respect.

"Is this deliberate?" I ask Naomi. "Or just a cultural thing?"

"It is both. We are told from early childhood on to think ten times before saying something once," she says. "Sometimes I forget and think only once or twice."

This causes a rhythm to Amish speech that still feels a little alien to me when I first walk into their homes. It takes me a few beats before I get used to it. Then I find myself settling in, enjoying the conversation, and yet again absorbing the peace I feel within an Amish home.

The first time my husband had a conversation with an Amish bishop, he thought that the long pauses in their conversation were the bishop showing displeasure with the fact that we had been invited to participate in their worship by one of the Old Order families in his district.

The simple truth, we found out later, was that this was how he spoke to everyone. He was a bishop with much responsibility. He took his role seriously and was revered by his church. His words carried weight and so he considered them even more carefully than most Amish before he spoke.

The Amish Pause is a serious attempt to apply the teaching of James 1:19–20: "My dear brothers and sisters, take note of this: Everyone should be quick to listen, slow to speak and slow to become angry because human anger does not produce the righteousness that God desires."

"Being trained to pause and think before speaking," Naomi says, "has many times kept me from saying things to my children or my husband in anger that I was later glad that I had not said."

I realize that I've seen Mary do this, too. When her children ask her a question, or for permission to do something, there is always that pause—a couple beats of silence in which she weighs her words. This pause tends to be missing from Englisch parents' conversation with their children and with each other.

The Amish seem to be more aware than most of us that the Bible teaches that the tongue is a powerful instrument. As it says in Proverbs 18:21, "The tongue has the power of life and death. . . ." This is heavy stuff, and it is not an accident that there are pauses in their conversations. They are weighing their words, and I have been told they often find themselves saying a quick prayer for wisdom before they speak.

This might seem like a small thing—a couple beats of silence before responding—but I think it might have more impact in child rearing than we realize. Words can destroy children . . . or heal them. Words can give them integrity . . . or put them behind bars. Death and life *are* in the power of the tongue. To pause more often in our parenting and weigh our words more carefully might be one of the greatest lessons we can learn from our Amish friends.

This is just one more way respect is *intentionally* built into the fabric of Amish culture. I've seen it exhibited in every Amish home I've visited. I have no doubt that it is one of the many keys to the contentment I see in Amish children.

Punishments and Consequences

"And if all else fails we spank."

—AMISH MOTHER

I have spent many hours among Old Order Amish families and have seldom observed so much as a raised voice between parents and children. I have never seen the children threatened with any kind of punishment.

On the other hand, I've often been in homes and at social events where the Englisch parent seems to be constantly threatening the child with punishment . . . and then not following through.

"If you do that one more time," I've heard Englisch parents warn a child on multiple occasions, "I'm going to . . ." After mentioning some sort of punishment, the parent continues with their adult conversation while the child ignores them and the warnings simply pile up unheeded.

Lots of warnings. Lots of words. No consequences. This is definitely not the Amish way. It is dangerous parenting that can sometimes lead to creating young adults who expect our legal system to have no consequences for them either. Unfortunately, the police are not as enamored of our children as we are.

My oldest son is a Human Resources supervisor for a major corporation. His most recent HR termination involved a young man who did not believe there would be consequences for anything he did or did not do on the job. There were several official warnings about coming to work late and extra-long lunch breaks, but the very next day the very same behavior would be repeated. Over and over. A recommendation for termination finally came and the young man was shocked. Apparently he had not really expected for there to be consequences.

The Amish do not have this same disconnect. As I've pressed my Amish friends for their advice on discipline, one thing has come up again and again. Each mother I've asked usually ends up saying, "Well, we do spank a little if it's really necessary."

This goes so strongly against the grain of our modern society that I hesitate even to mention it. There is no excuse for child abuse, ever, and yet there is a huge gap between actual physical abuse and a spanking in response to outright rebellion.

I did not want my three sons to ever experience any kind of hurt or pain. I wanted to wrap them up in cotton and protect them from every possible thing that could damage them. The last thing I wanted to do was to spank them.

They were good little boys and I was a good mother. My husband was a good provider and a protective father. He modeled spiritual servant leadership in our home while I watched over everyone's health and well-being. We prayed for our children and for each other. We took the boys to church three times a week, where they were taught by good teachers. Our sons had a good home in a secure house filled with love.

At least that's how I looked at things the day I decided to throw away the wooden paddle my father-in-law had given us and that my husband kept in a kitchen drawer.

I felt that owning the paddle was unnecessary. It had been months and months since the paddle had made its appearance. I reasoned that our boys would be good just because they were so loved.

Our paddle seldom got any real physical use. In fact, about the only time we ever resorted to it was when the boys would get too rowdy or tease one another too mercilessly, and then my husband would simply glance meaningfully at the drawer in which it was kept. That was usually all it took to calm them down. Just a glance.

Our middle son was quite the little artist. One day, he took the paddle out of the drawer and with a marker drew a sad face on it. Every time I opened that drawer, I would see the sad face and it would bother me. Here I was, such a good mother, and my husband was such a good father, and our home such a happy place. I believed we did not need to rely on such an archaic method of discipline as spanking.

I could almost hear music playing in the background as I dropped that paddle in the garbage. I did not, however, mention to my husband that I had thrown the paddle away. I had a sneaking suspicion that he would not be pleased, but I did it anyway.

Our two youngest sons, however, did notice it in the garbage. "Why are you throwing the paddle away?" the middle one asked.

Filled with love for my precious child, I explained that he and his brothers were such good children that I simply did not see the need for it anymore. He agreed with enthusiasm.

It didn't happen immediately, but it did happen. Slowly, over a period of weeks, I noticed an erosion of good behavior in our house. The boys became slower to obey. I found myself raising my voice to get them to pay attention more frequently.

One night, the two youngest were wrestling on the floor. The wrestling got more intense. My husband told the boys to calm down. They ignored him. My husband looked meaningfully at the drawer where the paddle had been kept and they ignored him. He told them to stop. They continued to ignore him. A lamp got knocked over. My husband told them that if they did not stop, he would be forced to get out the paddle.

The middle son, who was about nine at the time, made the very big mistake of laughing.

My husband shot out of the chair where he'd been reading and went straight to the drawer. I felt sick because I knew what he was looking for and that it was presently residing in a landfill somewhere.

"Where's the paddle?" he asked.

I explained that I had thrown it away because I didn't think we needed it any longer.

"You expect me to help you raise our sons, and you didn't think to talk to me about it first?"

I quickly apologized for not consulting him, but he was not happy.

"I'm going out to the garage to make another paddle," he said. "Then I'm coming back in and both boys are going to get a spanking. I won't be deliberately disobeyed by them."

What happened next has become one of our family's most oft-told stories, highlighting the difference between the two youngest sons' personalities. The youngest, Jacob, who was fascinated with anything to do with woodworking or tools, followed his father out to the garage, excited about getting to help his father make the paddle. The middle one, Caleb, who had made the mistake of laughing at his father, ran to his room and locked the door. I trusted my husband not to damage either child, so I did not interfere.

Soon my husband came back inside the house with Jacob trotting along behind him. They came to Caleb's bedroom door and my husband discovered that it was locked. He told Caleb that if he opened it *right now*, he would get only one swat. If he didn't open it, the door would be taken off the hinges and he would get a real spanking.

Caleb knew his dad would do exactly what he said. He immediately unlocked the door and apologized. The one swat he got was not particularly hard—but it made the point my husband needed to make: he was the dad and they would obey him or there would be consequences.

The biggest difference between my husband and me was that he came from a family of rowdy boys and I came from a family of obedient little girls. I had never been spanked. I was the kind of child who pretty much just wanted to make my parents happy. He and his brothers had been rough-and-tumble and needed a stronger hand. The paddle had hung right out in the open in his family home. Seldom used, but there.

The new paddle was put back in the drawer. Caleb drew another sad face on it, but I left it alone. To my knowledge, it was never used again, although there were times when my husband had to give that drawer a couple of hard looks.

Our boys could probably count on one hand the few times they got a swat on the behind, but the *possibility* was there. We had a rule. Spanking was reserved for two specific offenses: lying and deliberate disobedience.

They are grown men now and don't seem to be particularly scarred in any way. The paddle incident is told from time to time with laughter. Jacob still spends time with his dad making things in the garage.

It is universally agreed upon by the Amish people I've questioned that it is never right to spank in anger. A few mentioned the need to pray for wisdom before meting out punishment of any kind.

"I never spank my children when I'm angry," one Amish man said. "I'm too strong and I don't want to risk accidentally hurting them because of my own frustrations. I make sure I cool off and take the time to think things through. Sometimes I realize that my reaction is more about my anger than the child's need for such discipline."

The Bible says that to spare the rod is to spoil the child, and the Amish take that verse seriously; however, they are equally aware of a second scripture that advises against unfair and harsh punishment. Ephesians 6:4 says, "And ye fathers, provoke not your children to wrath; but bring them up in the nurture and admonition of the Lord."

Not everyone is comfortable with spanking a child—nor should they be. The debate about that is important, but beyond the scope of this book. However, even the Amish don't always insist on the necessity of spanking. One Amish father told me, "A wise parent learns his child—and what works with that child. God made each person different, and I believe families work best when the punishment is tailored to the individual child. For instance, one of my children automatically misbehaves whenever he starts feeling neglected and overlooked. That is a signal to me that he needs more time and attention from me—and I make sure I provide that before his behavior gets out of hand. Another one of my children hates shoveling manure out of the barn—really hates it—and I've discovered that knowing she might have to help me do so is a wonderful deterrent to any bad behavior."

However, one thing all Amish agree upon, spanking or not, is that bad behavior must bring about consequences or a parent is not doing his or her job. Whatever punishment is decided upon, it must be carried out consistently. Amish parents emphasized this to me over and over, and specifically mentioned inconsistency multiple times as a weakness they saw within the Englisch community.

The question, as the Amish see it, isn't so much whether to spank or not; the important thing is to make certain that there are appropriate and significant consequences when a child deliberately disobeys. They believe it is important to make sure that the child knows what the consequences will be, and knows that the parent will carry through with those consequences *consistently*. That, according to my friend, is how a child begins to understand that his actions matter, and how he will learn to choose more wisely next time.

Shunning

"Do not even eat with such people."
—I CORINTHIANS 5:11

Of course, the idea of actions having consequences in the Amish culture has such weight because consequences do not apply only to children. Adults are also held accountable. Amish children witness what happens when an adult intentionally disobeys the scriptures or the Ordnung.

If a person who has been baptized into the Amish church commits a sin, or does something against the rules of the church, they must show remorse and ask for forgiveness—which will be given. If an Amish person continues to deliberately disobey the rules of the church, they will be warned privately by a church leader that their behavior is not acceptable. If they continue in their wrong behavior, it will be made public and the church and family members will try to talk to them into once again following their church's beliefs. If they still don't change their ways, the church will formally shun them until they change and repent.

Shunning has been written about and commented upon so

many times in fiction and nonfiction about the Amish, as well as on television and in movies, that apparently it holds quite a fascination for outsiders. The success of such television shows as *Breaking Amish*, *Amish Mafia*, and a documentary on shunning that PBS's *American Experience* recently aired makes that fascination obvious. It is easy to for an outsider to see the act of shunning as punitive, judgmental, and mean-spirited.

The Amish see it differently. These are a people who believe absolutely in a literal heaven and hell. They will go to great lengths to save a loved one from hell, even if it is an emotionally painful process for all involved.

Various Amish churches differ in how strict or lenient they are, but all practice some sort of shunning when deemed necessary. Sometimes a shunned person will be allowed to come to a family get-together but will have to eat at a separate table apart from the rest of the family. Sometimes the church and family are not allowed to have any contact at all with someone who is shunned, even to speak to them on the street.

As harsh as this might seem to an outsider, the Amish see shunning as a loving tool to bring someone back into a right relationship with God.

Because there has been so much said and written about shunning in recent years, it is easy to assume that it is a frequent thing among Amish churches. My friend Leah, a member of the Old Order Amish who is in her late forties, tells me that in her experience, that has not been the case.

"The process of shunning is much rarer than most Englisch people realize. I have seen it happen in my particular church only once in my lifetime."

It does, however, happen, and the possibility of it helps keep

Amish people obedient not only to their interpretation of the scriptures, but to their Ordnung as well.

Scriptural basis for shunning is found in passages such as the fifth chapter of I Corinthians, in which the apostle Paul finds out about an immoral sexual relationship in that church and tells the members there to have nothing to do with the persons involved. In I Corinthians 5:11 he says, "But now I am writing to you that you must not associate with anyone who claims to be a brother or sister but is sexually immoral or greedy, an idolater or slanderer, a drunkard or swindler. Do not even eat with such people."

Another biblical passage involving the process of shunning is Matthew 18:15–17. "If your brother or sister sins go and point out their fault, just between the two of you. If they listen to you, you have won them over. But if they will not listen, take one or two others along, so that every matter may be established by the testimony of two or three witnesses. If they still refuse to listen, tell it to the church; and if they refuse to listen even to the church, treat them as you would a pagan or a tax collector."

There is also James 5:20, which reads, "Remember this: Whoever turns a sinner from the error of their way will save them from death and cover over a multitude of sins."

The application of shunning has changed somewhat in recent years for the more moderate sects of Amish. I am told by my Old Order Amish friends that their church will no longer shun someone for becoming a member of another conservative Christian church. Old Order Amish churches might allow, with regret, a family member to move "up" to the more liberal New Order church, the New New Order church, the "liberal" Beachy Amish, with their automobiles and electricity, or even the Mennonites.

Members might be allowed to change churches without shunning, but it will not be without social repercussions. Much pressure will be put on all members to stay within the ranks of the church in which they've been raised. Leaving is never an easy thing to do.

Other sects, like the ultraconservative Swartzentrubers, might shun a member of their church or family simply for becoming part of the Old Order Amish church, which they see as far too liberal.

For most of the intricately interconnected and socially dependent Amish, the idea of being shunned is nearly unbearable. It is regarded by some as a powerful tool to help keep the members of the church from becoming too worldly, and by others as an unfair weapon that holds people within a church against their will. Those who have been obedient tend to see it as a way to save their disobedient brothers' and sisters' souls and keep the church unified. Those who have been shunned see it as unfair and punitive. Sometimes entire families will leave the church to avoid having to shun a family member. Other families hold the line, hoping the loved one won't be able to bear the isolation and will come back into the fold.

Regardless of one's viewpoint on how and why the practice is applied, the shunned person is always one confession away from being forgiven and taken back into the church, no matter how long they have been gone or how badly their disobedience is viewed. Shunning, moreover, is only as powerful as the pull of the Amish community. It is not easy for someone to walk away from that kind of support and interconnectedness—even when it begins to feel unbearably legalistic and restrictive.

It is not an easy thing to be an Amish bishop or minister who is tasked with deciding when to shun a member. Few want the role. Most take up the mantle of responsibility reluctantly and prayerfully. When shunning is deemed necessary, most would prefer to walk away and ignore the problem—and yet they don't. Right or wrong, they face it and deal with it.

Children see this. They see that there are standards of behavior their parents also have to observe or there will be disciplinary consequences. The idea of "Do as I say, not as I do" is not acceptable in an Amish household. Parents also have to practice self-control and obedience. In general, they are not asking their children to obey rules that they, themselves, don't also have to follow.

How much impact does this have on Amish children? A lot. Seeing this consistent model of adult accountability to their church community and to God makes obedience and good behavior much more acceptable and understandable for an Amish child.

The Amish model of adult behavior having potentially serious social consequences runs counter to today's Englisch society, which champions individual freedom. This has to have an impact on children's ability to accept—or reject—consequences for their own actions.

What is an Englisch parent to do? Most of us really have no such accountability other than trying to obey the laws of the land. That's where it gets trickier. In many cases, the Amish don't have to think a whole lot about what they should do because many of those decisions have already been made for them, and have been for generations. As hard as it is for an Englisch person to obey the rules of the Amish, much of an Amish person's life can be lived somewhat by rote because most of their behavior is modeled after that of parents and grandparents. Things are just how they are and always will be. It takes discipline and obedience, but it does not take a lot of thought or creativity.

The simplicity of their dress, for instance, is appealing to me; were I to become Amish, I wouldn't have to think about how to dress myself. The choices would be narrowed down with almost no thought at all. The same applies to behavior. There would be many freedoms that would no longer be an option.

Englisch parents, to a large extent, get to invent their own lives and can be highly creative in doing so. Unlike the Amish who wish to remain Amish, we can choose an entirely different life than the one our parents lived or reject the lessons they passed on to us. Sometimes that is a very good thing. The people I respect most in this world are those who chose to become the turnaround generation in their family and through whom various abuses and hurtful behaviors stopped, as they gave their children a different and better childhood.

But this courageous outcome is not the result of telling children to "Do as I say, not as I do." It can only happen when parents choose deliberately to live with such integrity that it rubs off on their children . . . and then it can potentially change lives through several generations.

Amish Parenting Tips
for the Non-Amish

- Children need guidelines and structure applied consistently to their lives. Allowing them to do whatever they please can ultimately make them miserable.
- Instead of trying to make your children happy, focus on building persons of value. People of value and integrity tend to grow up to be happy people.
- It's fine to reward a child for their good behavior, but be careful not to attempt to bribe them into good behavior. Make them earn the reward, not lobby for it.
- Remember the marshmallow test. Children who develop the ability to wait will do better in life than children who expect immediate satisfaction.
- Speak to your children with respect and expect them to speak to you with respect in return. Put-downs between parents and children or between siblings aren't funny—they are damaging and unacceptable. Don't allow it. Start building respect early.

- Check your tone when you speak to and about your spouse. The kids will pick up on it and use the same tone against both of you. If you model respect toward your child's father or mother, your child will also have more respect for themselves. It is good to keep this principle in mind in divorced and paternity situations as well. If you have a problem with your spouse or your child's mother or father, make an appointment with a professional counselor instead of griping about them to your child.

- One way to model respect is to practice forgiveness—toward yourself, toward your spouse, toward your children, toward your own parents, and toward other people who might have hurt you. One of the most impressive things the Amish do is to nurture a culture of forgiveness. It takes ongoing practice and intentionality, but it creates a home and life filled with peace. It also creates a sense of security for the children in that family. They can rest in the feeling of grace that making a mistake is not the end of the world.

- Spanking isn't necessary, but consistent consequences are. As the Amish father said, "I discipline my child because I love him. If I didn't love him, I wouldn't bother."

· IV ·

Amish Work Ethic

Amish Work Ethic

"She knows how to help."

—AMISH TEEN, REFERRING TO HER FIVE-YEAR-OLD SISTER

On a recent visit to my friend Mary and her family, we enjoyed a lovely afternoon, and when it was time for dinner, Mary turned to one of her daughters and said, "I think we'll have pizza tonight."

For a moment, I wondered privately if I would be driving to go get it. Instead, Ellie, the sixteen-year-old, simply went in and busied herself in the kitchen. A short while later she called the men in from where they had been working in the barn.

Soon, we were sitting down to a meal of thick-crust pizza spread with homemade sauce from vegetables in Mary's garden. Just one slice was heavy with nutrients, and, like everything that ends up on Mary's table, delicious.

Their eldest boy had a project in the barn that he was anxious to get back to and did not linger long at the table after eating. Instead, he quickly excused himself.

"That Matthew works too hard," John said after watching his son grab his hat and head out the door. "I worry about him."

It was a simple statement, but it struck me that I had never, ever heard a non-Amish father worry about his teenage son working too hard.

Mary patted her husband's work-hardened hand. "Yes, he is just like his father. He works too hard, but he enjoys his work, and he is young and strong."

John nodded and went back to eating. I couldn't help but admire the way she soothed his worries and at the same time managed to gently praise him in front of their other children.

Most of us have heard that sitting around the supper table as a family, relating to one another at least once a day for a meal, has more to do with a child's good behavior and good grades in school than any other controllable factor. Watching this happy family conversing at the table made me believe it.

One of the girls used a rolling pizza cutter to halve a piece of pizza before scooting it onto her plate. This reminded me of something I'd recently discovered in my own kitchen.

"Have you ever used a pizza cutter to cut out egg noodles?" I asked Mary. "It works so much better than a knife."

One thing that Amish women all have in common is a desire to learn new and better ways to cook. They are constantly trading recipes, nutrition information, and cooking advice. I thought Mary would be pleased about this new labor-saving tip I'd discovered. Instead, she gave me a blank look.

"I've never made homemade noodles in my life," she said. "I wouldn't know how."

I was astonished. Not only was I eating pizza made from scratch, but a week's worth of fresh bread that had been taken out of the oven a couple hours earlier sat cooling on the counter. We had just passed around a dish of homemade applesauce made with fruit from a neighbor's apple tree that Mary had canned the previous autumn. We'd gathered fresh eggs straight from the hens' nests down in the barn right before supper. She informed me during dinner that for our breakfast pancakes we would have fresh maple syrup John and the children had tapped from trees on their own property.

If there was one household in the world I expected to make noodles from scratch, it was this Old Order Amish home.

"I have never even *known* anyone who made their own noodles," she added.

"I don't understand," I said. "I thought making homemade egg noodles was as Amish as kerosene lamps and buggies!"

"Perhaps." Mary shrugged. "But I've never made them. I've always just bought them from the store."

I noticed that Mary's daughters were listening to this exchange with avid interest. The father and remaining teenage son, however, had tuned us out and were concentrating on filling their stomachs. The making of egg noodles was not a subject in which they were interested, as long as noodles appeared regularly on the table.

"What dish do you prepare with these noodles you make with a pizza cutter?" Mary asked.

"After I boil and drain the noodles, I mix them with cooked cabbage, drizzle butter over them, and season the dish with salt and pepper. Then I crumble bacon on top. It's called Amish noodles and cabbage."

"I never heard of that dish," Mary said.

"But it's Amish!"

"Not to my knowledge," Mary said. "How did you come across it?"

I thought back. Where had I come across it? Not a cookbook. Not a family recipe. I snapped my fingers.

"It was at an art fair," I said. "There was a man with a food booth and the sign outside it said 'Amish Buttered Noodles and Cabbage.'"

"It sounds delicious," Mary said. "Perhaps this is a dish the Amish in another settlement fix, but I have never seen it. I have a good idea! Why don't you prepare it for our supper tomorrow night and you can teach me and the girls how to make it."

"I'd be happy to," I replied. "Do you have flour, butter, and eggs?"

"Plenty."

"I'll drive over to Troyer's Country Market and pick up some good country bacon and a couple heads of cabbage tomorrow," I said. "And then we'll be all set for supper."

I was delighted to have the opportunity to give back to this Amish family by cooking for them. Also, this was one recipe that I prided myself on. It nearly always got raves. I could hardly wait to see their reactions.

We made short work of washing dishes, which involved an assembly line made up of Mary, her daughters, hot tubs of soapy water, and sun-bleached dish towels. After the dishes were finished, we chatted long into the evening around the soft glow of a kerosene lamp. One of the girls led me to my bedroom in the back of the house with a flashlight, and left me with a small battery-operated lantern just in case I needed it in the middle of the night.

I was grateful for the light. Nights on an Amish farm when the moon is not full can be very, very dark. There are no house lights, no outside lights, just . . . night.

The next day, I left to go to lunch with an editor friend who lives nearby. We ordered dandelion gravy over toast, a local spring favorite consisting of stewed dandelion greens, chopped eggs, bacon, and a memorable sweet and sour sauce. Afterward, I stopped in at Troyer's and picked up bacon and a couple heads of cabbage.

When I got back to Mary's, it was time to gather eggs again. We went down to the chicken shed, shooed squawking hens away from their nests, and gathered another basketful, some of which were still warm from the nest. Then we went back to the house and created a small noodle-making factory on Mary's extra-long kitchen counter. Because they make all the bread their family eats, Mary has large plastic containers of flour.

"Oh, by the way"—Mary set a pot of water on the stove—"I invited my brother and sister-in-law to supper. I hope you don't mind."

"Wonderful." I grabbed a bowl and an egg. "A couple extra people won't be a problem. I can easily stretch this recipe."

"And their five children."

I paused in the middle of cracking the egg and stared at her. "Seventeen people?"

She lit the flame beneath the pot. "And Joyanne and Clay."

Nineteen people. I mentally doubled the recipe.

"Oh, and John's mom and dad will be coming as well. They heard you were cooking tonight and were curious about what you were going to fix." Mary glanced over her shoulder at me. Her eyes had taken on a telltale twinkle. It was the same expression I had seen on her face the day she planted geraniums in her husband's old work boots that had been left too long on her pristine porch. Mary had her own way of having fun.

"So far that's twenty-one people." I put my hands on my hips. "Just how many am I going to be feeding, anyway?"

"I don't know, exactly." She opened one of about two dozen kitchen drawers her husband had built beneath the long counter and handed me a rolling pin. "Some of the older cousins might bring a guest or two."

My enthusiasm for the task of noodle making plummeted. This meal was quickly getting out of hand.

"Then I should triple the recipe?"

"It might be a good idea," she said. "The men always have such big appetites, but just think. This could make a good story for one of your books. You could tell your readers what it is like to be an Amish housewife who needs to stretch a meal to feed a large family."

Quiet, tenderhearted Ellie watched me with sympathy in her big, brown eyes. "We will help. It will be all right."

It was already two o'clock and we were supposed to eat at six. I had just discovered that there were three (maybe four!) times the number of people coming than I had first been expecting . . . and I was also beginning to realize that I would be preparing dinner for a crowd with a five-year-old underfoot.

Mary's youngest, Susan, appeared to be fascinated with the idea of making noodles. She was already pulling the pizza cutter out of a drawer.

I knew that the older girls would be good helpers, but I was a little worried about the fact that Mary had not shooed Susan off to go play elsewhere. Instead, the little girl pulled a step stool up to the counter, climbed onto it, and stood there at my side, awaiting instructions.

I have to admit, the child was as cute as a bug's ear in her little Amish dress and little bare feet, but I was worried. In my experience, small children plus flour and eggs was *not* a good combination. The last thing I needed was to prepare a large, complicated meal from scratch with an eager kindergartner tucked beneath my elbow. It would have been rude to suggest the child leave, so I kept quiet about my misgivings while the other girls and their mother gathered around to watch.

I cracked three eggs into a bowl and whisked a couple of handfuls of flour into it.

"Why three?" Ellie asked.

"It's the number I've found to be easiest to work with on a countertop," I explained.

"How much flour?" Mary was jotting things in a little notebook.

"As much as it takes to make a stiff dough."

I sprinkled flour over the smooth countertop, dumped the dough onto the flour, grabbed the rolling pin, and began to roll it out. This was a skill that had taken some practice to master. Rolling out the dough with just enough flour between it and the counter was tricky.

Susan reached for the rolling pin.

"Oh, honey"—I held the rolling pin out of her reach—"let me make this batch. We'll find something else for you to do."

I seriously hoped that if I delayed long enough, she would lose interest and wander away. Well-behaved Amish child that she was, there were no temper tantrums or second attempts to grab the rolling pin. She patiently watched while I rolled the dough into a thin sheet.

When the dough was ready, she handed me the pizza cutter.

"Thank you, sweetie. I do need that now."

I ran the pizza cutter over the dough, making thin strips of noodles. The pot of salted water was already boiling and I lifted the noodles from the counter with a long knife and dropped them one by one into the boiling liquid.

Ellie handed me a wire strainer and in a few seconds, the raw egg and flour mixture had cooked into tender egg noodles that floated to the top. I skimmed them off and dumped them into a bowl, and Mary stirred a little salt and soft butter into them.

"Can we taste them?" Mary asked.

"Sure."

We each grabbed a couple with our fingers, blew on them, and sampled.

"These are really good." Mary wiped her fingers off on her apron and pulled on a sweater. "But I have a cow to be milked and outdoor chores to finish before everyone comes. The girls will help you with the rest of dinner."

With so many people coming, I was a little surprised that she was abandoning me and her daughters, but she seemed confident that things would work out fine, and I soon saw that she was right.

Ellie began slicing bacon into small strips. Twelve-year-old Marie stood at the stove watching over the frying bacon. Twenty-one-year-old Bessie sliced the large heads of cabbage into bite-size chunks. As soon as the bacon was crisp, we set it to draining on paper towels and ten-year-old Ida took over the slow cooking of the cabbage.

In the meantime, Susan stayed stubbornly at my side. Carefully, she started taking eggs out of the basket and lining them up on the counter in front of me.

I know how damaging criticism can be to a child, so I did the best I could to be patient with her. Ellie casually mentioned that Susan was quite used to wielding a rolling pin when she helped them make piecrusts. I noticed that the older sisters weren't at all annoyed with their little sister's presence. They treated her like an equal, so I adjusted my attitude and began to allow her to help.

It was then that I, who was supposed to be teaching, finally got the lesson.

That intelligent little girl already knew more about cooking than I did when I first got married.

The minute I stepped back and allowed her to do so, she expertly cracked three eggs into the metal bowl, whipped flour into them with a fork, spread the flour on the counter, and began wielding the rolling pin and pizza cutter. Her noodles were almost as straight as mine and the correct consistency. For safety's sake, I did not allow her to put the noodles into the boiling water, but otherwise she was capable of the entire process after watching once.

"You are such a good helper!" I exclaimed at one point. "Your mommy must be so happy to have a big girl like you helping in the kitchen."

She paused for a second, looked at me with a quizzical expression on her face, and then went back to making noodles without saying a word.

Little Susan's body language said it all. She was a woman on a mission. Dinner needed to be put on the table and I was wasting her time with idle chitchat and empty praise.

After mixing the noodles with large dollops of home-churned butter, we stirred the hot cabbage into the noodles, topped the huge, steaming mounds with crumbled bacon, sprinkled a little pepper on top, and the food was ready.

It was ready just in time, too. We had barely put the extra leaves into the large table and pulled it out to its full length before the extended family started arriving. Without being told to do so, Susan assigned herself the task of placing napkins and silverware at each place. Marie poured cold well water into glasses.

Ellie sliced the homemade bread. Ida opened two quart jars of applesauce, and dinner was ready.

Mary came in from her evening chores just in time to wash her hands, don a fresh white prayer *kapp*, and greet her guests.

I was flushed and sweaty from rushing around when John's brother-in-law came through the door. He grinned at me and said, "You look right at home."

I looked down at my skirt and saw that it was well decorated with flour. I ran outside to dust it off.

Twenty-six men, women, and children seated themselves around that long table. There was a short hesitation while John lit the propane lamp hanging from the ceiling over the table. He invited us to a silent prayer, and then we dug in to a feast of food and fellowship.

My mountain of "Amish" egg noodles and cabbage was quite a hit that night. We talked and laughed and told stories late into the evening. The children's faces were practically glowing all around us, enjoying the give-and-take of the adults' easy conversation.

With the exception of tired little Susan, who crawled up onto her mother's lap for a cuddle, and a couple of the teens who left to attend a Saturday-night singing (where Amish teens gather together to sing hymns and flirt a little), everyone stayed around that table for a long time. My noodles were discussed at length, along with the fact that none of the women had ever thought to make them from scratch.

A few days later, after I'd gone home, Mary called me from her phone shanty. She laughed and said that I had started quite a fad of homemade egg noodle making in their family. Her sister-in-law, always the health-conscious one, had even been making them from whole wheat. Mary also informed me that the family had given me a nickname. Did I want to know what it was? I was half afraid to hear it, but I said yes.

"We call you our 'Old Order Englisch' friend."

I could hear the smile in her voice and knew that my new nickname was meant as a compliment.

I have thought long and hard about the day Mary's daughters helped me cook dinner for the family. I learned several lessons from it. My words of empty praise to Susan still make me cringe. "Oh, what a big girl you are! What a good little helper you must be to your mother!"

Those words came easily to my lips because they are the same words I've used with my own children and grandchildren. I thought that's what a good mother and grandmother should do—praise and encourage children.

Instead, I now realize how condescending and belittling my words must have sounded to the child. Susan was no small force in the kitchen and she knew it. She had spent most of her short life watching, learning from, and helping her mother and elder sisters. She knew where things were. She had a good grasp of basic culinary skills. She considered herself an equal part of the group of women in her house who shared the chores, cooked the meals, and took care of their large family.

Instead of treating her with the dignity she deserved, I had nervously called her "sweetie" and "honey" at least half a dozen times that afternoon. Only later did I realize that I had never heard her mother use pet names for her, nor had her sisters done so. Mary and John respectfully addressed their children and each other by their given names, never by a diminutive.

Long afterward, it occurred to me that the entire time I was cooking with the five sisters, they had spoken to each other with patience. Little Susan was never once treated by her elder sisters as though she were a nuisance. Instead, they acted as though she was a valued member of the kitchen workforce, and she rose to the occasion. No wonder she looked at me with such puzzlement when I praised her. She wasn't anyone's little helper. Her name was Susan. She had company coming, a large family to feed, important work to be done—and she was good at it.

By the grace of God, I have managed to raise three fine sons, and I have been an intimate part of my granddaughters' and grandson's lives as they have grown up near us. And yet that evening with the Amish, I began to wonder if I have accidentally done my own children a huge disservice. When they were small, I woefully underestimated their ability to be working, integral parts of our family. I began to suspect that this might be a big part of the Amish secret for raising happy children. They don't just allow their children to help contribute to the family, they expect it—and so do their kids.

I'd always assumed when my children were young that it was my job to provide for them, pick up after them, clean up after them, cook their meals for them, wash their dishes and clothes—at least until they were much older than competent, five-year-old Susan. Had I shortchanged them?

I decided to keep probing to find out.

The Importance of Chores

"Chores help a child feel like they are a *necessary* part of the family."
—AMISH MOTHER OF SEVEN

Many years ago, our middle son was taking karate lessons. He was eight years old. Karate was good exercise, helped him work off his energy, and he loved it. He even got pretty good at it. One day he was participating in a local competition. It was just a small event, but it was a big deal to him. He practiced and practiced. For several weeks, my life was filled with a little boy jumping, kicking, and leaping around the house while I did my work. I thought he was adorable and often told him how wonderfully he was doing.

The night of the competition, he did well, but so did another little boy. In fact, the two ended up in a tie. The instructor did an interesting thing to break that tie. He took the boys aside and asked each of them to tell him quickly what chores they did regularly around their home to help their family. The other boy rattled off several.

My son stood there, unable to think of one thing. Because of that, and only that deficiency, he was awarded second place.

There was a very good reason he couldn't come up with any

chores to tell the instructor about—he didn't have any. I had found it easier to simply do things myself than to take the time to teach him.

I will never forget how angry he was while we drove home from that competition.

"Why don't I have chores?" he demanded. "You should have been giving me chores. I felt stupid standing there not having one thing I could say that I did to help my family."

He was right. We had failed in a major way. We had taken him to soccer games and baseball practice, Scouts and church, itty-bitty basketball practice and karate lessons, but we had not given him the dignity that would have come with being a part of contributing to our family's needs.

After the noodle incident, I called Mary to ask her about how chores play a role in their family life. We started off with some chit-chat, catching up. Mary had finished feeding all her farm animals and was ready for a nice visit. In the past, she and I have laughed about our mutual fascination with each other's lifestyles. I tell her that she is living the alternate life that sometimes I wish I had . . . a large family of beautiful children, lots of wonderful relatives living nearby, kerosene lamps and horses and buggies and homemade bread cooling on the counter. It frequently looks idyllic.

On the other hand, Mary says she sometimes wonders what it would be like to spend all day every day writing books for a living. She enjoys writing poetry and has allowed me the honor of reading some of it. Because that is her image of the way I spend my days, I know she'll be interested in hearing about my latest venture.

"I've decided to get a Jersey milk cow, Mary," I tell her. "Just like yours."

She laughs so hard that I'm afraid she'll fall out the door of her phone shanty.

"Oh!" she says, and I can picture her wiping tears of laughter out of her eyes. "What a good joke you are telling me!"

"I'm not joking. I'm going to do it."

"But, Serena, you are a writer, not a dairy farmer."

"I'm only going to get one cow. I can learn."

She starts giggling again.

"What?"

"Oh, nothing. It's just that I can't wait to see you trying to milk a cow in the middle of winter in the snow! John and I might have to hire a van just to come down and watch."

Her laughter is infectious, and I'm certain my hoped-for Jersey cow will soon be a topic of discussion with her friends. There are times when I suspect that my main role in my Amish friends' lives is as a source of entertainment and amusement to them. I have a suspicion that at get-togethers and work frolics they are saying the Pennsylvania Dutch equivalent of "You girls aren't going to *believe* the question Serena asked me the other day."

"I have to do this, Mary. My husband's doctor says it would be a good idea for him to drink milk that has not been pasteurized."

"This is that nutrition doctor you were telling me about?"

"Yes."

She sobers. "And how is your husband doing?"

"His last blood test showed that his cancer numbers have gone up."

Mary and I had met a few weeks before my husband collapsed while splitting firewood. Eleven months of excruciating pain and seven doctors later, he had been diagnosed with a rare and hard-to-diagnose form of multiple myeloma—bone cancer.

A bone marrow transplant had put him into remission, and he was relatively healthy and able to work again, but we were doing everything possible to keep the cancer from coming back. A doctor at the hospital where he had the transplant had developed a nutrition protocol to fight off his own late-stage cancer and had ended up helping thousands of other patients with it. My own research had turned up the health benefits of drinking pure raw milk, and the nutrition doctor, who is a part-time farmer, had confirmed it.

I had done some reading and discovered that there was no rhyme or reason to the various state laws regarding raw milk. Some allowed it to be freely sold and purchased in stores. Some allowed it only if it was purchased at the actual farm. Some allowed it only if one bought into a "herd share" program—which means buying milk from a cow that you technically own, but that a farmer feeds and milks for you. The herd-share program was the only thing allowed in Ohio, but there were legalities within legalities about that to the point that some small-time Ohio farmers had been arrested in sting operations that uncovered their illegal sales of raw milk.

My sisters and I had been raised on raw milk from our family cow and I had read that there are healing enzymes in it that are missing from pasteurized milk. I also had a friend with a science background who attributed at least part of her recovery from leukemia to its beneficial effects. I therefore had little patience with Ohio's laws, especially since the selling of raw milk was completely legal just one state over, in Pennsylvania. This is why I was exploring the option of buying my own milk cow.

"Oh, I am so sorry." All traces of laughter in her voice have disappeared. A husband's health is a serious matter. She begins giving me seasoned, professional advice about choosing and keeping a cow.

"If my seven-year-old can milk a cow," she encourages me, "then *you* can milk a cow."

It may have been my imagination, but I thought I heard an element of doubt in her voice.

"Wait, your seven-year-old milks cows?" I ask. Wasn't that terribly young to be given such a potentially dangerous task? What if the cow kicked? Most seven-year-olds I know couldn't be trusted to reliably feed the dog, let alone deal with a large animal.

"Of course," she says. "How else will she learn?"

The Amish, she reminded me, start teaching a child to help with small chores when they are two years old. Why? Not because a two-year-old can actually be any real help but because that child, in the Amish way of thinking, needs to start feeling like a necessary, contributing part of the family. Mary can rattle off a list of tasks that are appropriate for each year of a child's life.

A few days later, I received a handwritten note from her in the mail. She had thoughtfully given me a list of chores and the ages at which she and other Amish mothers had their children performing them. I found the list enlightening, charming, and very Amish. It was written exactly as follows:

Chores for children:

Feed and water hens, gather eggs (if no silly rooster is in the flock)—Age 4

Carry wood for heat stove—Age 6

Carry out ashes—Age 10

Milk a cow—Age 7 to 12 (depends on muscle strength)

Feed horses—Age 6

Bed horses—Age 10

Mow lawn—Ages 6 to 12

Pull weeds—Age 4

Wash main dishes—Age 4

Wash pots and pans—Age 10

Sweep kitchen floor—Age 5

Set table—Age 4

Do laundry—Age 11

Rock baby—Age 5

Bake a cake—Age 8

Bake cookies—Age 7 (if oven mitts are worn)

Fetch mail—Age 5

Harness a pony—Age 7

Harness a horse—Age 12

I remembered Susan sitting in a child-size rocking chair when she was only five as she held an Englisch baby her elder sister was caring for. The baby had seemed a little large for such a small girl to handle, but Susan had taken the job quite seriously.

At first all of these ages seem to me a bit young for the size of the chore. I've been in Mary's basement. She does laundry on an old-fashioned wringer washer fueled by a gasoline engine, an appliance that even most adult women wouldn't know how to use these days. An eleven-year-old seems awfully young to be taking on such a large job.

But then I remember how vigilant Mary is with all her children. None of these chores would be done without supervision until the child was proficient, but the training would begin, and the chore would eventually be done well and become yet another skill a child could count themselves as possessing.

Allowances

"Allowances for children don't really compute in the Amish mind."
—PAUL STUTZMAN

After reading Mary's list of chores and the ages at which she assigned them, I made a note to ask her to explain about how the Amish handle allowances. How much did they give each child, and what did that child have to do to get an allowance?

"And how much does each child get for allowance?" I asked the very next time I visited Sugarcreek.

"Allowance?" Mary asked, clearly puzzled. "They do not get allowances."

"You don't give them money each week? Maybe for the chores they're assigned?"

"We make it possible for our children to earn some money, but we don't give them some set weekly set amount. We certainly don't pay them for their assigned chores."

No allowances? I remembered the intense and detailed negotiations over allowances I'd had with my sons when they were young. We had tried several methods, and none of them had worked very well. We tried to tie their allowances to doing the few chores I started assigning them when I thought they were old enough—but our lives were busy and so were theirs. Their chores were left undone some chaotic weeks, but they'd come to depend on that bit of money and it didn't seem fair to penalize them for our own lack of household structure.

"A child needs to do helpful things just because she's part of the family," Mary said. "Not be paid for doing something she should be doing for the family anyway."

Paul Stutzman confirmed this for me. "Allowances for children don't really compute in the Amish mind." He tells me the Amish expect their children to work, and they do not offer their children financial rewards every time they turn their hand. Chores are simply part of learning to contribute to the family. Instead they introduce their children to the concept of earning money early in life in order to instill in their children a sense of responsibility about finances, one that runs throughout their culture and follows the children into their adult lives.

Amish children don't expect allowances, I discover when I press my Amish friends, though sometimes they will be rewarded financially by their parents for good behavior or for working harder than usual.

Leah, my Amish friend who homeschools her youngest three daughters, wants them up and ready for breakfast by six in the morning. Instead of yelling at them to get up, she simply encourages the development of self-discipline by giving each of them two dollars for every morning that they are ready on time without her having to remind them.

"It is possible for them to make as much as fourteen dollars a week during the school year," she tells me. "And they really like making that money. But they do have to buy their new dress material out of it, and shoes, and anything else that is extra."

"And that works?"

"It's worked well for me," she says. "Most mornings they are dressed and ready before six. It is also helping them learn to be good managers of the money they earn. That is something every child needs to learn."

I'm impressed. My method of getting my boys ready was more along the lines of standing in the doorway yelling that they were going to miss the bus, or, on one especially frustrating day when the oldest one would *not* get out of bed, throwing a bucket of cold water on him.

"Do your girls ever sleep in regardless?"

"Sometimes," she says. "But then they have to watch their sisters get paid and they get nothing, and they don't like that at all!"

When I ask Naomi how she teaches *her* children about frugality and earning, she tells me of one fun way she has developed for them to earn their pocket money.

"I don't pay them to do every little chore," she says. "They have to learn to do things just in order to contribute to the family. But there is a game I play with them when I need to have the house cleaned really well."

"What kind of a game?"

"I save up quarters," she explains, "and then I hide them all over the house. The children must move things around to sweep and dust and to put things away. If they find a quarter, they get to keep it. If they don't find all the quarters—I count them before I hide them—I tell them that the house must not be clean yet and they have to go back and work some more."

"And they like this?"

"Oh yes," she says, laughing. "Sometimes they even ask me to please make a quarter-cleaning day for them."

I am impressed with her creativity. "Did you make this game up yourself or is it some kind of an Amish thing?"

"I didn't make it up," she says. "I read about it in *Family Life*, so there are probably other Amish mothers who do it, too."

"Do you want to know how I teach my children to hang up their coats when they come inside?" she asks.

"I sure do."

"They have learned that if their coats are hung up, they sometimes find a surprise in their pockets, like a small candy bar or a dime. Not always, but sometimes." Naomi's eyes are alight with enthusiasm. "Oh, they are very good about hanging up their coats ever since I started doing that! I never have to remind them."

I find myself wishing Naomi had been in my life and had taught me this trick when I was raising my sons. Things would have gone much smoother at our house.

Amish parents don't see the use of rewards as simply encouraging good behavior, but as a way of inspiring a strong work ethic in their children.

"Amish parents don't hand their children an allowance for merely existing like some Englisch parents do," Paul tells me, "but they do try to come up with ways for them to *earn* it."

"What ways might they earn it?"

"I picked wild blackberries as a kid and sold them to neighbors," Paul said. "I know of one Amish father who helped his young son create his own small business by helping him build a chicken coop. He provided the finances to buy the chicken wire, the chicken feed, and the laying hens. As the boy began to sell eggs, he paid his father back a little at a time for the money he had invested in his business."

"Did the father need the money that badly?" I am surprised the dad would ask for the money to be paid back from the small amount the child probably earned.

"No," Paul explains. "He didn't, but he knew his son needed to learn the realities of owning his own business."

I realize I'm starting to get to the heart of the entrepreneur training that made it possible for the Amish in our area to create thriving businesses in places where I did not expect a business to prosper.

"In what other ways do children learn how to earn?"

"A family who runs a roadside produce stand would expect their children to participate in the planting and hoeing, and it would be common for the children to be assigned a small garden plot of their own where they could grow vegetables to sell. They could probably keep the money for themselves." Paul pauses to think of other ways he's seen Amish children earn. "Children whose parents make their living weaving baskets will help their parents in the family business, but they might also be allowed to make a few baskets of their own to sell.

"Girls start babysitting for neighbors and family members as soon as they are old enough, and they also help clean houses. It is not unusual for a new mother to hire a younger sister or cousin to come for a few weeks to help cook and clean when a new baby is born. I also know of one boy who made his pocket money by raising and selling rabbits."

I'm impressed by how industrious they are, but still, I'm extremely surprised when, a few days later, Mary tells me that her three eldest children, who have part-time jobs, routinely hand over their entire paychecks to her and her husband, and that this is the norm for most Amish families.

"*All* of it?" I ask.

She nods.

"How long will they do this?" I ask.

"Usually until they are twenty-one or married," she says. "A little longer if they are unmarried and still living at home."

"You're saying that your three oldest children just hand you their entire paycheck without complaint?"

I'd heard of a few Englisch parents charging rent, but taking every dime the son or daughter makes seems excessive.

"Yes, and then my husband and I give them enough money for them to take care of their own needs."

When Mary first explains this practice to me, I am astonished, but apparently she and every other Amish person takes it for granted. It is the way things are and always have been. The reasoning is that she and her husband took care of the children until they graduated from eighth grade. Now it is time for them to pay their parents back.

"Besides," Mary explains, "it is not a good thing for young people to have too much cash in their pockets. It can lead to too many temptations, and many Amish teens make good salaries."

Later, I run this new information past Paul. "Don't the children resent this arrangement?"

"Not when every Amish family they've ever known has done the same thing," Paul explains. "It is another example of *uffgevva* in the Amish culture. The good of the family is more important than the individual who is earning the money. An older teenager's salary as a carpenter or a grown daughter's salary as a salesclerk, when added to the family finances, can make a big difference to the comfort and security of the family."

Paul goes on to explain that instead of resenting the expectation of their contribution, teens seem to take pride in the fact that they are now old enough to help pay off the family farm, add an addition to the house, or simply help put money into the family's bank account for a rainy day. Again, he reminds me, this is a good example of the concept of *uffgevva*, a concept in which they've been steeped since birth.

The Job Market

"Amish kids show up on time, they work hard, they have a lot of common
sense, and they don't steal. . . . What employer wouldn't want that?"

—JOYANNE HAM, B&B OWNER

Joyanne sometimes employs Amish girls to help her with the
housekeeping and cooking involved in running a B&B, and she
has been quick to point out the advantages of having an Amish
employee—even if that employee is still a teenager.

"They have a great attitude, a lot of skill, and they actually
know how to work," she says. "In fact, it's a little hard sometimes
for an Englisch teen to get hired around here when employers
have the choice of so many Amish young people to hire instead."
She shrugs. "Amish kids show up on time, they work hard, they
have a lot of common sense, and they don't steal. They're not covered in tattoos and most of them are sober and drug-free. What
employer in their right mind wouldn't want that?"

I know a lot of Englisch teenagers who work hard and have a great
attitude, but I think the transition to becoming part of the workforce
is sometimes a little rougher on them than someone raised Amish.

For one thing, an Amish teen enters the workforce at a much younger age. In the eighth grade they are already preparing themselves to go to work because they know that will be their last year of school. They know that at around fourteen years old, there might be training and certification classes to take but that their childhood is basically ending.

The earliest many Englisch teens enter the workforce is at age sixteen, when they get a driver's license. Many don't have any real-world work experience until after high school, or perhaps even after college.

Basically, the transition from being at home and in school to becoming an employee tends to be a little easier for Amish youth. Often, the standards of work they've had to meet while working within their own families are already as stringent as many Englisch employers expect from them. That fact is reiterated when I talk to the men at Keim Lumber Company, based in Charm, Ohio, which employs more than four hundred workers. At present, approximately 75 percent of those workers come from an Amish heritage. Since the Amish forbid formal education past the eighth grade, roughly three-fourths of Keim Lumber's workforce does not have a high school education or any computer training when they are hired, and Pennsylvania Dutch is their first language.

None of this was a problem for the owner, Bill Keim, who built his successful company from the ground up. He also had only an eighth-grade education. Pennsylvania Dutch was his mother tongue as well.

It is hard to describe Keim Lumber Company to those who have never seen it. The place is unique. I was told repeatedly by locals that I needed to go visit, but I put it off because I couldn't imagine what a lumber company could possibly have that would be of interest to me. I envisioned stacks and stacks of, well, lumber.

Then one day while visiting the Homestead Restaurant in Charm, with plenty of time on my hands, I walked across the road, entered Keim Lumber, and stood inside the front door gaping. My first impression was that the owner had gone overboard in using the most beautiful woodwork and flooring possible.

There were many different kinds of hardware, all sorts of tools, both electric and nonelectric, as well as rare woods from all over the world. It was a sort of carpenter's paradise combined with an upscale kitchen and bathroom store. It was so lovely that I took pictures.

Ivan Miller is a Mennonite and works in employee development at Keim Lumber. Because of his lifetime friendship with Paul Stutzman, he agreed to take time to meet with me. I wanted to ask about the Amish work ethic from a major employer's standpoint. When Amish children grow up and get jobs, what do they bring to the workplace? Are they easier to work with or more difficult? Does the eighth-grade education create a noticeable learning gap? How hard is it to run a large, modern business when much of your workforce has never before touched a computer? Are Amish children prepared for life outside the home when they go out to look for jobs?

On the day that I went to meet Ivan, my husband came with me. We deliberately arrived early to give my husband a chance to check out some tools that he needed. It was the first time he'd ever seen the place.

"Did I exaggerate?" I asked after we'd wandered around for a while.

"Nope," he said. "Not in the least. I'm in awe."

One of the most unusual sights one sees while visiting Keim Lumber is Old Order Amish men in traditional beard and dress, sitting behind computers, clicking away at keyboards. To Englisch eyes, that sight is a bit disconcerting. The Amish, on the other hand, are quite matter-of-fact about it. They are accustomed to using tools at work that are not allowed at home. Computers are simply another tool to them. I've discovered that in the Amish mind-set, it is one thing to *use* something that is forbidden, but an entirely different thing to *own* it.

Paul also came that day, and we were soon seated in a small conference room with Ivan and two other longtime Keim employees who happen to be Old Order Amish. Both were serious, well-spoken, and dignified family men. Lester appeared to be in his early forties. Rudy was a bit younger.

I thanked them for their time and we engaged in a few pleasantries while I pulled out a notebook in which I'd jotted down questions.

"What are the difficulties that you have to deal with as you employ those with so little formal education?" I asked. "Do you ever have trouble training Amish workers in new technology?"

I was aware that my question might sound rude, but getting the answer to this is one of the main reasons I'd gone there. None of the men seemed to be offended by my question.

"No," Ivan said. "In fact, we've found just the opposite. The Amish employees don't seem to have any ceiling at all on what they can learn. It's as though they don't worry about how difficult something might be, or the fact that they don't have any training in it. They just go ahead and master it. The Amish are great problem solvers."

"But what about computers? Certainly that must have presented problems."

"Not really," Ivan explained. "They pick it up pretty fast. For instance, we had one Amish teenager working for us who became so interested in our computer system that he taught himself to be proficient in it. In fact, it turned out that he had taught himself more than either he or we realized."

"How's that?" I was scribbling notes.

"Well, one day there was a major problem with our computer system and we called in an outside professional to fix it," Ivan said. "The computer expert worked on our system for quite some time before he finally gave up. He told us the problem was beyond his ability. Just about that time, the Amish kid, who had also started tinkering with the system, came in and told us that he'd fixed it. We investigated and found that it was true. He had. He didn't seem to realize that he wasn't supposed to know what he was doing—he just went ahead and did it."

"My youngest son works as an IT computer specialist," I told him. "I have some idea of how complicated his work is. I'm surprised that someone with no formal training and so little education could teach himself to do that."

"I hate to say it," Ivan continued, "and, as a Mennonite, I'm not against formal education, but some of the most difficult people I've ever had to train were also some of the most highly educated. It's as though they had spent so much time in school, they somehow lost their common sense."

I saw Lester, who is an Old Order minister, nodding in agreement. "Common sense can take a person a long way."

"You have to understand something else," Ivan continued. "There is a huge difference between the way Keim Lumber does things involving computers and the way the corporate world does things."

I was intrigued. "How so?"

"It involves the software. In the corporate world, the software they use tends to be something designed to control their workers. In fact, the software is usually marketed with the basic assumption that the company is employing dishonest workers. At Keim that isn't our mind-set. Until someone proves otherwise, it is assumed that all our workers are honest. If you don't trust a member of your team, you can't work with them, so why even try?"

"So you are telling me," I said, "that you believe the Amish that you hire are more honest than those who aren't Amish?"

"Don't get me wrong." Ivan seemed a little uncomfortable with my interpretation of his words. "We have plenty of very honest Englisch people who work here, and I can't say that every Amish person is honest—although I wish I could. Let me just say that overall we have found most of our employees to have a great deal of integrity."

"What about sick days and coming in late?" I asked. "Seventy-five percent of your workforce drives a buggy, walks, rides a bike, or catches a ride to work with someone else. How do the Amish stack up against Englisch workers when it comes to promptness and dependability?"

"They do really well," Ivan said. "These are people who know how to work, and more importantly, they *want* to work. They've been brought up this way. They're not going to jeopardize a good job by being late if there is any possible way to avoid doing so."

"The Amish workers I hired back when I managed a restaurant," Paul added, "were rarely late getting to work in spite of slower forms of transportation, and they were very good about showing up. I found I could almost always depend on them."

"Do you think that is because they get more satisfaction from their work than Englisch workers?" I asked.

"Perhaps," Paul said. "The idea of 'finding yourself' is not an Amish concept. To the Amish, a job is a job. Work is work, and to have work is a good thing. If it pays well enough to support their family, an Amish person is content."

"So, in your opinion," I asked the three Keim employees, "what do the Amish do right to instill this wonderful work ethic in their children?"

As so often is the case in conversations with the Amish, there was a respectful pause while everyone pondered the question.

"In my family, it is my wife," Lester answered after a short silence. "She is the one who is with the children all day and she teaches them constantly. I'm amazed at what she accomplishes. She always goes the extra mile in making sure they know how to do things."

Rudy nodded in agreement. "That's the way it is at my house, too. My wife has taught our children from the time they were little how to help out the family."

"In Amish society," Paul added, "the children get up early and have chores. It gives them a purpose for existing. In Englisch society, they get up and watch cartoons. Reality versus make-believe. It definitely makes a difference in their work ethic as well as their worldview."

Lester leaned toward me, his expression earnest. "The impact of all that training teaches children what it feels like to think that 'I am a useful, helpful, necessary part of my community and my family.' That is a good feeling, and it is an important gift to give a child."

"There is a word I would use to describe how the Amish raise their children," Ivan said. "That word is *intentionality*. Very little is left to chance in an Amish home. They *intentionally* teach their children how to work and they *intentionally* teach their children the value of honesty."

"And as a culture," Lester reiterated, "we're able to instill this work ethic primarily because of the dedication and hard work of our wives."

Keim Lumber is a busy, thriving workplace and I know it is a sacrifice for these men to take time out of their workday to meet with me. I thanked them for their time and left, pretty sure I had my answers. The Amish work ethic does not happen by accident. Amish children are *intentionally* taught how to work by the words and examples of their parents, and that ethic is modeled by everyone else within their culture. This pays off in their employability, even without formal education.

If they are going to survive as a culture, it has to be this way. These are a people for whom welfare or government aid is not considered an option. Historically, they have neither contributed to nor accepted Social Security to help cushion their old age. An Amish man assumes he will keep working until he can no longer hold a hammer or walk behind a plow. They do not seem to begrudge this fact. Work at any age not only provides income, it gives a person a feeling of purpose.

I used to wonder if the Amish are just naturally born competent businesspeople. My Amish friends are constantly coming up with creative (and usually successful) ways to add to the family finances. Abram works in a woodworking shop and raises livestock to sell on the side. Naomi and Luke's oldest boys work full-time as carpenters. Leah, in addition to doing a great deal of gardening, has a small business in which she turns people's sentimental material or garments into memory-type stuffed animals. ("It was so hard to cut into that lovely wedding dress," she once wrote me. "But the customer really wanted it made into a teddy bear.") Another daughter babysits. Another one makes rag rugs on a floor loom. One of Mary's girls trains horses. An Amish woman near my home makes beautiful hand-painted greeting cards and has quite a brisk trade before Valentine's Day when young Amish men line up to buy her special creations for their sweethearts.

Some of the Amish people supplement their incomes with writing. At the yearly book signing at the Gospel Bookstore in Berlin, there are always several tables filled with Amish people selling self-published memoirs, cookbooks, or books about local Amish history that they've researched and written. Like the teenage Amish computer expert at Keim Lumber, they don't care that they have no real training in commercial writing—they just go ahead and do it and some of them are doing it very well.

"Do you discuss family finances in front of your children?" I ask Mary. "Do you let them know how much money you have or don't have?"

"John and I are open about our finances with them up to a point," Mary says. "I don't think small children should have the pressure of worrying about their parents' finances—but the older children know basically what their father makes, and how much we have in our savings account. We allow them to hear us discussing the wisdom of certain purchases, and how much to give to someone when there is a need in our community. It is a way of teaching them about handling money. That is why we are open with them about why we make the financial decisions we make."

It is clear to me that Amish children are expected to pull their weight at home and in their surrounding society at a much earlier age than we Englisch tend to expect. The result is that they do not allow an unnatural childhood to be fostered in their adult children. The Amish are a competent, skillful, hardworking people. This does not come about by accident, but by a deliberate nurturing of an admirable work ethic, and it may be one of the most important things we can learn from Amish parenting.

The Importance of Fun

"Having fun together is an important part of discipline."
—AMISH MINISTER

After our visit to Keim Lumber, Paul Stutzman and I continued to discuss how the Amish go about instilling their impressive work ethic into their children. Paul, with his heritage firmly rooted in the Amish tradition, is one of the most disciplined people I know. In addition to holding down a demanding job, he's hiked the entire 2,200-mile Appalachian Trail and biked solo across the United States in spite of harsh conditions that would have made most people give up.

"What did your parents do right?" I ask him. "What was different about your childhood that enabled you to accomplish what you have—or were you just born disciplined?"

"What I remember most is how lazy I was as a kid." He chuckles. "I hated having to work, but they made me do it anyway."

"How?"

"By example, for one thing. Everyone around me worked hard. It wasn't possible to be lazy for long in our family. Plus, I liked to eat. We grew or raised most of what was set on the table and it didn't take me long to see a connection between hoeing corn and having a full belly. I complained as a child, but they expected me to complete the task anyway. I remember looking down the long, clean rows of vegetables after I had finished hoeing them, and realizing my hard work was truly contributing to my family's needs. Mom and Dad would tell me I'd done a good job and that feeling of satisfaction was important to me."

One of the things I realized in this conversation with Paul is that the work assigned to him as a child might have felt like drudgery, but it was never used as punishment. He knew that the work he was doing actually contributed to the good of the family.

I see the effects that this truth has on my friend Mary's home life. In spite of having so many children, no electricity, lots of livestock to care for, and relatives and friends coming and going daily, her home still runs so smoothly that she never seems to be frazzled or particularly overworked, nor do her children. With everyone pitching in, and not a lot of emphasis on an abundance of material possessions, there always seems to be plenty of time to simply enjoy life and one another.

Her children's contributions always pay off in some small way. Work in the garden and the kitchen creates good food. Work with the livestock produces either gain in food products or family finances. Getting morning chores done quickly means that their mother will have more time to do something interesting with them, such as sewing or quilting, or work that involves an art project such as making greeting cards. The last time I was there, the youngest one had dragged in containers of dirt and rocks and was happily building container gardens in the middle of the basement floor while her mother calmly supervised and hung laundry up to dry.

An Amish minister told me that the Amish consider play, oddly enough, part of teaching their children to work.

"Having fun together," he told me, "is important. It is one of the main ways in which we reward our children for good behavior. There must be a balance between work and play or a child will become rebellious."

There is wisdom in this, but from what I've seen, the Amish definition of play is sometimes very different from how the Englisch see it. Basically, there is a smaller gulf between "work" and "play" for the Amish than there is for many of us.

For instance, when a family is getting ready to host church—the Amish do not have central church buildings, but take turns worshipping in one another's homes—it is usual for a group of women to get together to help the host family clean and prepare their house. Even the walls will be washed or painted. Food will be brought for lunch. Children will run all through the house and barns playing and helping. Because the adults are chatting and laughing and enjoying themselves as they work, the children feel free to have fun as well.

Making homemade ice cream is considered play. Milking the cow that gives the cream for the ice cream, however, is usually considered a chore. Picnics are an enjoyable part of a family's life. Fishing in a nearby creek or pond is play—but the frugal Amish will probably clean and eat the fish for supper.

A young girl might consider learning to sew on her mother's treadle sewing machine a form of play. As I mentioned before, letter-writing is a favorite activity and many Amish girls develop lifelong friendships with their Amish pen pals.

I mentioned to Mary that I'd once read about a young Amish boy who had been made to plow with his father's four horses when he was only eight. I asked her if she didn't think that was abusive. She laughed and said that most eight-year-old Amish boys would beg for the chance to do such a masculine job.

Hunting is a favorite activity among the Amish men and boys. This was a surprise to me, because I thought the pacifist Amish would not own guns. I was wrong. They keep guns in their homes, but those guns are never to be turned against a fellow human being. Bringing home venison for the freezer is something else entirely and seen as just good sense with deer so plentiful.

One thing that a lot of Amish families do for fun is add to their family birding list. The Amish are great observers of the natural world and are famous for their birding skills. Most Amish children are able to identify many different kinds of birds and always keep their eyes open for an unusual one. When they do spot one they've never seen before, it is identified and added to the family's list of birds.

Then there is what we would consider real play. You can almost tell which Amish families have teenagers living with them because of the volleyball net that's set up in the summer. Trampolines for the little ones are quite prevalent. Pony carts are considered great fun for little boys and girls, as well as good training for later when they will need to handle horses. Winter play involves jigsaw puzzles, reading books together, and sledding.

Of all the activities the Amish enjoy, traveling has to be near the top. To make it even more enjoyable (and frugal), they tend to travel in groups. Going to visit relatives in other Amish settlements is a favorite activity, greatly anticipated and written about in detail in their newspapers.

When Paul Stutzman describes his childhood, he doesn't dwell on all the hard work. It tends to be more about nostalgia of all the good times he had with his family. He describes early mornings in his grandmother's kitchen watching breakfast eggs sizzle in her cast-iron pan, playing outdoors with his cousins, eating popcorn on the front porch at night with his family. There seems to have been enough hard work to teach him what he was capable of accomplishing, and enough play to make his memories of his childhood such that he can't keep from grinning as he recounts all the joys of growing up in that environment.

When I look back on my own childhood, the happiest and most vivid memories are of the times my hardworking mother decided that enough was enough, abandoned her housework and laundry, and took the afternoon off to go on a picnic. Sometimes she made this decision in the middle of winter with snow on the ground, which made it even more fun because it involved carrying hatchets and making campfires, and wrapping up in heavy blankets while we watched the snow falling around us. As a woman in her nineties, she told me that she had only one regret as a mother. When I asked her what it was, she said she wished she could have played with us children more, but that it had seemed like there was always just so much work to do. I reassured her that she had done a wonderful job as a mother.

As I look back at raising my own children, the memories that are the happiest and most vivid to me are the times when I abandoned all my responsibilities and worries and simply *played* with them. It didn't seem to matter whether or not we had any money to spend. In fact, one of their happiest memories is the day when we drove from Detroit out to a state park, pretended we had been stranded in the wilderness in the middle of winter, and had to build a shelter with nothing but our bare hands. We gathered fallen limbs and wild grapevines, and spent the day weaving a strange-looking makeshift shelter that probably made a few state park employees scratch their heads when they came across it.

Like my own mother, my greatest regret as a mom is that I did not make myself push worries and work aside and play with my sons more. For me, too, it always seemed like there was just so much work to do. I now remember none of the work—while those days of play shine bright in my memory.

I once read a letter to Ann Landers that has haunted me for years. A mother wrote in complaining about how her kids didn't want to have anything to do with her after they were grown in spite of her having done a long list of things for them. The tone of martyrdom in her letter was so thick, I found myself sympathizing more with her neglectful children than with her. Ann Landers responded with "Yes, you may have done all those things, but were you ever any fun?"

What I have seen within the Amish community is that they work very hard, but they also have a lot of fun. Recreation seems to be deliberately built into their enjoyment of being a family. This is no doubt another reason Amish families tend to be so emotionally bonded.

"It is easier to teach a child to work if they know there will be the reward of play," an Amish minister once told me.

One never hears an Amish person speak of "burnout," but it is a word I hear a lot in the Englisch world. I wonder if it is because the Amish, in spite of being some of the hardest workers I've ever seen, are also experts at incorporating a balancing amount of "play" and social interaction into their lives. By example they teach their children to do the same.

Amish Parenting Tips for the Non-Amish

- In general, kids are capable of being taught more skills than we realize. Take the time to help them become competent. Give them the gift of feeling needed and necessary to the well-being of the family.
- If at all possible, find ways for them to earn and manage money.
- Stop handing out empty praise. Kids are smart enough to know better. You cheapen your relationship with them by endlessly bragging on them.
- Reward their work by taking the time to play—even if it is nothing more than a picnic in the backyard.

· V ·

Technology

Technology

"Have you ever watched *Little House on the Prairie?*"
—YOUNG AMISH GIRL

I was spending the night with my friend Naomi and her family. The dinner dishes were washed. The eldest son had gone to bed in order to get up early for his construction job. Naomi's husband, Luke, was reading. Naomi was mending a little dress. An older daughter was writing letters. I was reading a children's book aloud to Naomi's three littlest girls, who were sitting grouped around me on the floor.

It was a pleasant evening and I was thoroughly enjoying myself. I finished the book I was reading to them.

"Have you ever read the Little House on the Prairie books?" one of the little girls asked me.

"Not only have I read all of them, last year I got to visit Laura Ingalls Wilder's house!"

This caused a flurry of excited questions. What was her house like? Where was it? And most important, what did the kitchen look like?

I was able to answer all the questions in detail because I had been as in awe of being in Laura's home as Naomi's daughters were.

Then one of the girls asked a question I had not been expecting. "Have you ever watched the television show, *Little House on the Prairie?*"

It seemed an odd question for a small Amish girl. "Why?" I asked. "Have *you* ever watched it?"

All three girls nodded.

The older sister smiled, and explained. "We have a battery-operated DVD player," she said. "And some Englisch friends bought the whole Little House series for us for Christmas last year."

I tried not to show too much surprise over the fact that they owned a battery-operated DVD player, but Naomi read my thoughts and looked up from her sewing.

"It's not something we usually talk about," she said. "But I do allow the girls to watch Little House stories on rainy days when their work is done, or when we've been snowed in for a long time. I feel like those shows teach good lessons."

"I couldn't agree more," I said.

"We also have the Waltons series." There was a touch of defensiveness in her voice as she told me this. "But that is all I allow them to see. Both shows teach good principles that I think strengthen a family."

Even though owning a battery-operated DVD player doesn't quite fit with my ideas of what you would expect to find in an Amish home, when I thought about it more, I realized it wasn't so terribly surprising. Battery-operated devices aren't forbidden by their church, and, knowing Naomi, I am certain that the time in front of the DVD player is limited and the experience is used as a treat, not something that consumes their lives. I am also certain that she and her husband carefully discussed whether or not these two series would strengthen their family or weaken it before they accepted them.

The Amish do not shun all technology. But they are, as with most things, very intentional about how they allow it into their lives. The more I talked to my Amish friends about it, the more I became convinced they have something to teach us about this as well.

Quality Time
Versus Quantity Time

"Children need quality time ... and lots of it."
—CHILD PSYCHOLOGIST

My husband and I were attending a workshop on the family a few years back. The lecturer, a child psychologist, began his topic with these memorable words: "Parents frequently ask me what is the most important—*quality* time with their children or the *quantity* of time they spend with their children," he said. "They wonder if the small bits and pieces of time they have with their kids are good enough if they make that time special enough. So, I'm here tonight to answer that question. Quality of time or quantity of time?"

I listened intently. I'd wondered about that same question and discussed it with my friends. Quantity or quality? Was I finally going to get the answer?

After a long pause for emphasis, he answered his own question. "After many, many years of counseling kids, I can answer that question absolutely. Children need quality time . . . and *plenty* of it."

There was a ripple of laughter in the audience, but the psychologist didn't smile. It wasn't a joke. Children, he continued, are hardwired to need lots of time and attention from those who are raising them.

Unfortunately, having time to spend with one's children is apparently at a premium in today's society. According to the Nielsen Corporation, the average child spends 1,680 minutes per week watching television—approximately thirty-two hours per week. Meanwhile, some sources claim that parents spend less than thirty minutes per week in real conversation with each child, while other sources claim that parents spend less than five minutes per week talking with each child.

I have trouble believing these figures. There must be something wrong with those statistics. I can understand how statisticians could monitor the amount of television watched—but I think it would be extremely difficult to get an accurate average of parent-child conversations. However, there is one inescapable fact—many children evidently spend many more hours passively watching television than they spend actively engaged with their parents.

This statistic is only about television, which is no longer the only time dump. Internet and social media usage is off the charts, and with these distractions, even more time is taken away from parent-child relationships because parents' time is also being sucked up by all the electronic entertainment and communication media now available. I think most of us can agree that excessive technology use at the expense of personal time with one's child is a poor investment.

A friend of mine recently told me about something she saw at a doctor's office. A mother had a small son who was desperate for her attention. Unfortunately, the mother was engaged in texting. Not only was she ignoring him, she was shoving him away each time he tried to climb into her lap. His desperation for her attention escalated along with his disruptive behavior, but the texting continued. Finally, the nurse called the mother's name and they exited the waiting room before there was a complete meltdown.

Bad attention, apparently, is better than no attention at all. Children will act out—sometimes desperately—in order to get the attention they crave.

Dr. Catherine Steiner-Adair, a psychologist, sees many parents, teens, and younger kids in her clinical practice in Massachusetts. She recently wrote a book titled *The Big Disconnect: Protecting Childhood and Family Relationships in the Digital Age.* Steiner-Adair interviewed one thousand children between the ages of four and eighteen, asking them how they felt about their parents' use of mobile devices. She says the language that came up over and over again were words like "sad, mad, angry, and lonely."

She says that when parents focus on the digital world at the expense of their children, there can be deep emotional consequences. In so doing, we are behaving in ways that tell children they don't matter, they're not interesting to us, they're not as compelling. One girl said, "I feel like I'm just boring. I'm boring to my dad because he will take any text and any call any time."

On a school trip to New York, our seventeen-year-old son got separated from his school group. This was before everyone had cell phones, and there was no way for him to contact his group. People were all around him, going about their business, but he didn't know anyone and no one knew him. He told me later that it felt so strange, this feeling that no one could see him, the feeling of being completely invisible because no one cared about him. He said he had the strangest desire to climb up onto something and start screaming just so people would notice that he existed.

He finally found a phone booth and had enough pocket money to call us. We made some phone calls, and within a few minutes, our son got an unexpected ride in the backseat of an NYPD squad car while the police located his group. He was fine, but the terrifying feeling of being invisible haunted him for months.

Sometimes I've wondered if that feeling is one of the reasons some kids start acting out in various dangerous ways. They have experienced that feeling of being invisible for far too long.

Television, computers, and cell phones. Most Amish do not allow these items in their homes or lives, nor do they allow themselves the luxury of being connected to the power grid. They do not believe that God will strike them down for indulging in these things. They do believe, however, that owning this technology can cause enormous damage to a family, not only because of some of the ungodly things that appear on the internet and television, but because it distracts the parents from the important job of raising and teaching their children.

I've spent several nights with my Old Order Amish friends and one thing that is noticeably different from our Englisch culture is that the family tends to spend the evening together in the same room. At dusk, kerosene lamps or a more powerful gas-powered light will be lit in the living room. Whereas electricity tends to distribute the family all over the house, a lack of electricity draws them closer together, kind of like moths to a flame.

The Amish amuse themselves in the evening in different ways. Sewing, reading, making crafts, doing puzzles. Babies and toddlers are a delight not only to the parents but to the entire family.

When one doesn't have TV or computers, playing with a small child or teaching an infant to take her first steps is welcome entertainment even for older brothers and sisters.

A lack of personal attention is something few Amish children experience, even within large families. From the time they are born, they are surrounded by a group of close-knit relatives and friends who view children as blessings from God. The Amish, because of lifestyle sacrifices they make, simply have fewer things to distract them from giving their children the attention they crave. Instead, the children are constantly being observed by their parents as they learn to cook, sew, craft, and tend to gardens or livestock.

So, how is a busy, overworked parent supposed to get all this extra time to observe and spend time with their children?

Taking a good, hard look at one's particular time dumps or one's lifestyle might provide the answers. If a long commute is eating up huge chunks of a parent's life, it might be wise to think of alternatives. If the mortgage on a house is making overtime a necessity, it might be a good idea to downsize. If a job is so draining that all a parent wants to do when coming home is veg out in front of the TV, it might be wise to start actively looking for a different way to provide for the family.

Sometimes the time dump is simply a day-to-day choice. My husband and I struggled with two things in spending enough time with our children. A minister is basically on call at all times, and working with people's problems can drain the life right out of a person. I know there were times when he just didn't have one more ounce of caring to give. Somehow, he always managed to dig deep into his emotional wells of energy long enough to make certain the boys knew that his highest priority was not the people of our church, but his family.

I loved to read. There were plenty of times when the latest novel I'd checked out of the library was a whole lot more entertaining than reading *One Fish Two Fish Red Fish Blue Fish* aloud for the hundredth time to my toddler, but I knew it was important to put my book down, so I did.

One of the biggest challenges Englisch people face today in raising their families is that there are so many fascinating things to distract us from spending time with our children. Just like the mother busily texting in the doctor's office while her little boy clamored for her attention. I know one mother who frequently spent as many as twelve hours a day in chat rooms, and many dads who prefer engaging in a hobby on the weekends over spending time with their kids.

Here's one thing I know absolutely: even though it might take discipline to make yourself gear down and listen to a child prattle on about her latest LEGO creation or some small thing that happened at school, a parent who stops listening will create a child who stops talking. Obviously, this can have tragic consequences.

On the other hand, one of the greatest gifts parents can give themselves and their children is to raise them in such a way that once they are grown, they aren't just sons and daughters anymore, but close friends.

This does not happen by accident.

A life is built one small decision at a time. It's like a house laid brick by brick. Every time I disciplined myself to lay down an interesting novel and pick up Dr. Seuss, I added a small brick to my relationship with the child. Every time my husband turned away from writing a sermon to mend a small boy's toy or to play yet another game of Candy Land, he was carefully placing another brick in the secure wall of his relationship with our sons.

Anyone who thinks raising children doesn't involve making thousands of small personal sacrifices of time is deluding themselves. We went through many things with our sons when they were growing up and made many mistakes, but one of the things we did right was to make sure the conversation with them never stopped.

Sometimes it took some creativity.

When my middle son was a teenager and going through a time of withdrawing into his bedroom, I tried many times to get him to talk to me about what was going on in his life. I was worried about him. I wanted him to sit down at the table and talk to me while I fixed dinner, the way he used to as a little boy, but he wasn't interested. He resisted every effort to start a conversation. It finally hit me that I was trying to pull him into my world. Since this wasn't working, I decided to enter his.

I remember the feeling of having a million things to do and not time enough to do them all, but I had a strong feeling that I'd better not let my son spend another day in his room alone after school listening to music, which was all he seemed interested in doing. So I knocked on his bedroom door and asked permission to listen to his music with him. He was suspicious—this was odd behavior on my part—but he tentatively agreed.

I lay down on his bedroom floor, closed my eyes, and just listened—really listened—to his music for about an hour. Finally I got up, told him that I had enjoyed it, and I went back to my work. The next time I asked permission to listen to music with him, he showed a little more enthusiasm. He played several songs for me, telling me what he liked about them, apologizing for some of the words used in the songs, and telling me details about the music groups he admired.

There were many thing I would rather have been doing. I did not love listening to his music, but I did love him. Those small sacrifices of time opened up a conversation between us at a time when communication was imperative.

It is easier for the Amish to listen to their children because they are with them more and face fewer distractions. A father and son cleaning out the barn together have time to talk. A mother and daughter cutting out a dress pattern or washing dishes together have time to talk. A toddler in a house where there is no television or computer can be highly entertaining and will enjoy—as most toddlers do—being the center of attention.

Elsie, an eighty-two-year-old Amish grandmother, has a simple answer for how to spend more time with one's children. She speaks softly, trying not to sound too judgmental. "It might help if Englisch people turned their television and computers and cell phones off more often. God gives us these children as a gift, and they are with us for such a short time. Every minute is so important."

I remembered an experiment we did with our boys, and I had to agree.

We had just moved to an area where television reception was spotty and we couldn't afford cable. I had allowed my sons to watch entirely too much television while I was distracted by sorting and packing for our move and they had regrettably grown used to watching as much television as they wanted. Those first few days in our new home with nothing to watch caused them to be quite distraught.

To placate them while we got ourselves settled in our new home, my husband and I made a deal with them. If they could make straight As for that six-week school period, we would buy an antenna for the house.

I observed some interesting behavior over the course of those six weeks as our family went off television cold turkey. I had to conclude that we had an addiction. We went through withdrawal when our passive entertainment disappeared, and it wasn't just the boys suffering—my husband and I were, too.

It wasn't bad during the day. We worked hard and were pretty well occupied. But in the evenings we were tired and longed to relax in front of the tube. It felt like we were suddenly forced to live in a vacuum until bedtime. We hardly knew what to do with ourselves. Evenings, when we had formerly watched TV while the boys played, worked on homework, or sat watching beside us, began to feel very, very long.

We played board games, but I often had an eye on the clock as I privately grieved over some favorite program we were missing. We read books, but it felt so strange just to be sitting there in silence, reading together. We talked, but we ran out of things to say. I remember driving home at night from some function, seeing televisions flickering in the windows of other people's houses, and being envious.

TV had been a sort of comfort food that we snacked on each night until it was time for bed, and it had been taken away from us. I felt jittery. Nervous. I hadn't realized that evenings could feel so long.

It took a couple of weeks for that feeling to diminish and for us to actually relax and enjoy paying attention to one another. We began to work at the kitchen table on the boys' homework with them instead of haphazardly working on it in bits and pieces in front of the television. To my shame, I realized that we had fallen into the habit of helping our sons with their homework only during commercial breaks.

We began to have weekly "old-fashioned nights" on Saturday evenings. We'd light a couple of kerosene lamps, make popcorn, and sit around the radio listening to the old-fashioned live radio show *A Prairie Home Companion*.

At the end of six weeks, our sons brought home straight As for the first time ever. I had begun to enjoy our relaxed, family-oriented evenings and was surprised to find myself dreading the toxin of TV entering our home again. But we'd made a promise to the boys and we needed to keep our word.

"Your father and I will go pick up an antenna tomorrow," I told them. "A deal's a deal."

That's when we got a surprise.

"Could you wait a little longer before you do that, Mom?" our middle-school child asked. "I kinda like getting straight As."

"My teacher asked my class today how many kids thought they could live without television," our seven-year-old informed us. "And I was the only one who raised my hand."

"How did you feel about that?" I asked.

"I was fine," he said. "But I felt sorry for the other kids."

We did not have television in our home again until the boys were grown. Instead, I started a writing career, and my husband and I and our sons spent four years hand building our dream house. Our youngest took lessons from an elderly Appalachian basket weaver and learned not only how to weave baskets, but what side of a hill to choose a sapling from, what kind of sapling to choose, and exactly how to create his wooden strips from raw material.

In other words, our boys had quality time with us and plenty of it, and my husband and I found ourselves shaking our heads at all the time we had once wasted on . . . nothing. Our Amish friends, had we known them then, could have told us about all the time we would save—time that could be spent on more important things—if we gave up television, but we had to learn it for ourselves.

I am convinced that one of the biggest reasons Amish children seem more content is that they seldom need to whine or misbehave in order to get attention.

They already have it.

Deciding

"I've tried to teach my son well, but still I worry . . ."
—AMISH FATHER OF A TEENAGE SON

Images of Amish country are familiar to locals and tourists alike: farmers in fields or little children on a wagon or buggies trotting past tidy gardens or a line of laundry blowing in the breeze. Those images are everywhere in the gift shops and tourist attractions and can be found down almost every road in any Amish settlement. But sometimes even those of us who spend much time in Amish Country catch a glimpse that startles us.

One day, when I was driving in the steady traffic of busy downtown Berlin, Ohio, I saw a teenage Amish girl guide her bike expertly along the line of heavy traffic. Full skirt billowing, strings on her cap flying out behind her head, she seemed quite untroubled by the flow of cars, SUVs, and semis that blew by her as she pedaled along. She was even relaxed enough to be guiding her bicycle with only one hand on the handlebars.

There was nothing unusual in that picture. Bicycles are a primary mode of transportation in Amish country. They hold their own on all the highways, from the small dirt township roads to the busy state thoroughfares. One can see people of all ages on bicycles, from four-year-olds to grandpas.

But this glimpse of Amish life was one of those that made even a local look twice. The girl was driving with one hand because her other hand was occupied—holding a cell phone to her ear. Whatever phone conversation she was having seemed to make her oblivious to her surroundings. She was as wrapped up in her conversation as the teenage Englisch boy who maneuvered around her in his car, also driving with one hand and talking animatedly into his cell phone.

The Amish do not shun all technology, and Amish teenagers during rumspringa—their "running around" period—are generally allowed to use some technology until they make the decision to officially join the church. But even for members who have been baptized into the church, rules for what is approved vary by community, and the rules can change as the community's needs or technology changes.

I know of some enterprising Amish who have created lucrative businesses for themselves by selling "Amish computers," which can do everything regular computers can do . . . except access the internet. Many Amish books have been written on what is basically a word processor. Some Amish sects who do not allow cell phones do allow the use of phone shanties and appreciate the existence of answering machines. It makes it possible to have access to a telephone without having it rule one's life. The same thing applies to the internet. I know of one Amish family who sometimes has to access the internet to run a small home business. They use the computer at a local library to deal with their business issues. It surprised me the first time I received an e-mail from an Old Order Amish reader, but she was matter-of-fact about it. She had accessed the internet to contact me through the very library where she had checked out my book.

The Amish with whom I've spent time are far from ignorant about technology; rather, they are deliberately selective in how they use it.

Every generation has its challenges, technology-wise. Paul tells me that when he was small, television was considered the biggest issue, the most alarming threat to young, developing minds. His family did not have a television and as a child he felt deprived. But now he says he looks back and remembers constantly being out in the woods, at the library, riding his bike, or being with friends and is grateful for his upbringing.

To the Amish, television was seen as an evil influence to society in general, but it has not been much of a problem for them because their homes did not have electrical outlets to plug televisions into. If anything validated their decision to stay unconnected with the world through being attached to an electrical utility, it was the advent of television. Whether or not to have TVs in their homes was pretty much a no-brainer. When they viewed it through the filter of how it would affect the family, the leaders gave it a resounding "no."

These days, there are other technological evils the various church leaders must discuss, deal with, pray about, and make rules for. Unfortunately, the technology of today is evolving so fast it is hard to keep up.

For a while the biggest debate was over cell phones. It was a difficult decision for many communities, because an argument could be made for a cell phone being important to the family. It was easy to see how a family business could be greatly enhanced by a cell phone, or could be used to call for help in life-and-death situations. Even the Amish know the value of calling 911. Motherhood could also potentially be enhanced with a cell phone. A pregnant mom could have quick access to a midwife. An Amish mother with three or four teenagers running around could keep better track of her children.

I was surprised the first time an Amish mother confided that she and her husband shared a no-frills cell phone.

"Aren't cell phones forbidden in your church district?" I asked.

"Well, sometimes we cheat a little," she answered. "We don't use it to sit around and chat. We use it only so that our children who are working can call if they need us."

I was sure they had wrestled with the decision to own one. On one hand, they desired to obey their church. On the other hand, there was the deep-seated Amish desire to keep in close contact with their family.

I was even more surprised when, after their church had discussed the dangers of cell phones even further, the family quietly gave theirs up and went back to their phone shanty and an answering machine. In their case, the community decision to keep this technology out of their lives trumped their very natural desire to be more easily available to their older children.

Time passed while various Amish churches weighed the pros and cons of their members' owning cell phones. Some allowed them in very specific business or risky health situations. Some did not allow them under any circumstances, and life went on.

Then the iPhone was invented, and it was as though a small bomb had gone off in the Amish community. Not only could these phones take photos and videos—which is forbidden in nearly all Amish settlements—but they allowed immediate access to the internet, and they did not involve electrical outlets. What's more, these devices were easily purchased and easily hidden.

The Amish youth who were old enough to have jobs, and who had not yet joined the church, no longer desired a simple cell phone. They wanted all the bells and whistles.

Today, if you ask any Amish person what they considered the greatest threat to their culture, you will probably get the same answer: the "picture phone." They are probably right.

Through the "picture phone" Amish young people are being exposed to things they would never have experienced before, many of which can be extremely toxic. What's more, parents now have much less ability to control or even realize how much information and entertainment their young people can access.

Even the most conservative Amish sects are struggling with this problem of cell phones to some extent. In the past, even those who didn't have phone shanties at their homes could at least access a pay phone if necessary. Now public pay phones are disappearing at an alarming rate, making the possession of some sort of cell phone almost necessary.

Teenagers, both Amish and Englisch, are pulled by a powerful desire to keep in touch with friends. Some Amish youths are becoming so involved with their games and social media that they are practically unaware of what is going on in their family.

The Amish have traditionally allowed their young people a small amount of freedom during their dating years, but it's becoming an increasingly slippery slope. As a frustrated Naomi said about her daughter who bought an iPhone recently, "What did Facebook do with my daughter? She hardly talks to me anymore."

The breakdown of family communication and togetherness is

one reason many Amish church districts are taking a hard line on cell phones, in addition to television, video games, and computers.

One Amish father told me, "Even if we were permitted to have computers, I would not have one in my home. I know myself, and I know that I would be on the computer in the evenings instead of enjoying my family. We have a good time together and I want to enjoy it while my children are still home."

This generation of the Amish is having to make hard choices requiring wisdom and discipline. They've made hard choices before and have survived, but "picture phones" may be the most worrisome invention yet.

Hard on the heels of internet usage in the Amish mind is the problem of pornography. The Amish are not immune, nor are they unaware of the possibility of it being accessed through what they call the various "picture phones."

One Amish minister confessed to me that it was his greatest worry—the fact that his nineteen-year-old son now had access to anything he might want to see through his smartphone. I was surprised that the Amish father brought pornography up at all in mixed company, but the Amish are not a people who have ever buried their heads in the sand when it came to possible harm to their families. They can easily see that the cell phone has opened up a Pandora's box of possibilities.

A friend of ours, Dr. Lou Butterfield, is trained in addiction counseling, and he partners with his son, Ryan, who is a certified sexual addiction therapist. They have produced a DVD series called *The Mouse Trap*, about the devastating effects of pornography on individuals, marriages, and families. He says that videos of sexual activity have been scientifically proven to be far more addicting than mere photos. Some people, in trying to achieve a greater "high," fall into a downward spiral of viewing increasingly perverted acts and become unable to stop without professional help.

"Internet pornography is private, it's free, and it has been proven to have the same 'kick' of dopamine that is released with taking crack cocaine," Dr. Butterfield tells us.

The first time I heard Dr. Butterfield speak, he was counseling not only adults but also children as young as seven who have developed a full-blown addiction to pornography.

He advises strict guardrails against internet usage and much parental supervision. As I talked with him, I couldn't help but think about how the Amish, in general, don't have to worry a whole lot about a seven-year-old becoming addicted to internet porn. There just isn't the access.

Far from being a backward people, the Amish have good reason to be suspicious of new technologies that the Englisch invent. Instead of immediately embracing each new thing that comes along, they wait and watch. If they see that the technologies are having a bad effect on our families, they will choose not to allow it into their own homes. Whereas in our culture, most of us tend to want to be first in line for any new technological gadget, the Amish's slow deliberation and debate over accepting new things has created a cushion of protection around their families.

Many people seem to believe that the Old Order Amish are still virtually living in the 1800s. This is not the case. They are a people trying to figure out the best way to live their lives in the twenty-first century, and they are experiencing both successes and failures—just like the rest of us.

Fewer Wants

"We had the *best* Christmas!"
—AMISH MOTHER OF SEVEN

One of the many benefits of a home without a television was recently reinforced to me when I got a letter from my friend Naomi, enthusiastically describing her family's Christmas. Her letter simply overflowed with joy over their lovely day. She has seven children, all of them still at home. With her and her husband, there are nine people beneath that roof.

To my knowledge, they are not struggling financially, so I was a little surprised to read that the entire immediate family, from the youngest to the parents, exchanged names for gift-giving. With her permission, I'm including the letter she wrote describing her family's Christmas:

> *Good morning Serena,*
>   *Greetings from my easy chair beside the fire. It doesn't make for the best hand-writing, but it sure does feel good with it only 11 degrees outside and the wind howling.*

It's not daylight yet. I just got done with morning chores outside. Milked the cow, fed five calves, one got a bottle of milk, fed laying hens and a bunch of roosters that are in danger of hitting my frying pan. Mm-mm. And I put out more sunflower seeds and suet for my feathered friends. Lots of different varieties come. I'm begging one more kind to come and that is the brilliant Red-Headed Woodpecker. Three other kinds of woodpeckers come but not him. I know they are around. We see several in the summertime down in the woods. Maybe it's too windy here atop the hill for them.

Luke and David have left for work. Jacob is feeding heifers, pigs and dogs and horses. The girls are still all snuggling under covers. Once they get up, there will be hungry ponies to look after and school work. My oldest, Fanny, needs to go to the restaurant at 11:30. Sixteen-year-old Hannah will clean a neighbor's house this forenoon. This neighbor man had open heart surgery on Monday. I think he is 52. This was unexpected.

Holiday season is behind us. We had a nice Christmas. I had Luke's name and gave him a hat. He had my name and gave me dish washing racks, a drain board, and an outside water spigot. David got smithy tools, Fanny got ice skates, Jacob got a basketball, Hannah got clogs and rubber stamp supplies. Frieda got a saddle pad and bag. Sarah got a dolly. Rebecca got a book, a rubber-band gun, and a flashlight.

I've got sewing to do now. The girls will help me. Yesterday I cut out five pairs of pants. The girls started a five-hundred-piece puzzle. I love puzzles. They keep me from my important work sometimes.

With all this snow, it's good coasting weather. We've got a big piece of plastic which used to be a feed bench. After we opened gifts and had our Christmas meal, we went for some thrilling rides. Six

of us could all get on it at once. We put on some old couch cushions to
ease the bumps. Fanny and Hannah went ice-skating last evening.
They are probably sore. I hope your husband's back is feeling better.
Bye. Naomi

I reread her letter, and was not sure that I was understanding everything correctly, so I called and left a message in her phone shanty to call me back. When she did, she was a little surprised at my question: Did each person truly receive a gift from just one family member?

Yes, she told me. Their family exchanged names. Why was that a surprise to me? They each got a nice gift. No, she and Luke did not give presents to each child, just whatever name they drew.

"What about their grandparents?" I asked. "Didn't they get any gifts for the grandchildren?"

She laughed at my question. "Do you have any idea how many grandchildren our parents would have to buy for if they got a gift for each grandchild?" she said. "Luke's parents have sixty-three grandchildren. Mine have thirty-four. It just wouldn't be possible."

"What about Santa Claus?" I asked. "Did your younger children get any Santa Claus gifts?"

There is a momentary silence on the other end of the phone.

"Well, we don't really go in for Santa Claus around here much," she said.

Even though I feel comfortable with our friendship, and have learned a great deal about Amish beliefs and ways, every now and then I accidentally trip up. Of *course* they don't go in for the whole Santa Claus idea. A culture that would prefer their children read about Amish martyrs rather than "fairy tales" would not.

I turn the conversation into a different direction. What other sorts of gifts did she feel were appropriate for children? One thing I'm pretty certain about is that the gifts her children received will not at all resemble the ones many of the Englisch children I know opened at Christmas: Nintendo 3DS, Wiis, laptops, iPads, iPhones, XBoxes, Playstation 4s, and personal TVs for their rooms seemed to have dominated.

Naomi tells me that the few toys her younger children get are simple, old-fashioned, and have stood the test of time. Baseball gloves, bats, and balls. The ever-popular jigsaw puzzle. A coloring book involving barns and farm animals. A new box of crayons. Board games. A new puppy or kitten. A child-size clothesline with tiny clothespins with which they can "help" mother. A child-size rolling pin. Plenty of dolls, mainly old-fashioned baby dolls, but no Barbie dolls. Building blocks. Plastic horses and farm animals. Maybe a new lunch tin for an older teen who "works out."

Naomi is always helpful. A few days later I received several pages torn out of an "Amish" catalog, primarily the entire toy section. She wrote on the top: "These sheets are very much Amish toys—plus lots of dolls."

I looked through the advertisements and picked out several more items she left out during our initial conversation: chess, checkers, a freestanding globe that is also a bank, marbles, a jump rope, Etch A Sketch, a spinning top with a small train inside, a rubber-band airplane, a jack-in-the-box, a wooden work bench with functioning tools, tiny tractors and play livestock trailers, handcrafted (by Amish woodworkers) wooden farms involving fences, a hay bale elevator with crank, horse stables, and large toy Clydesdales complete with vinyl harnesses.

At the top of a page containing a hundred-piece set of small plastic farm animals, she wrote, "Makes great church toys!"

For the first time in a long while I saw Wooly Willy—the picture I spent hours playing with as a kid, using a magnetized pencil and metal shavings to decorate Willy with hair and beard.

A kaleidoscope and a horseshoe puzzle, lawn darts. Monopoly was not in the catalog, but board games entitled Horse-Opoly and Farm-Opoly are advertised. Memory games and table tennis sets. Heirloom-quality wooden Mancala and tic-tac-toe boards. A thirteen-piece play tea set and an eight-piece stainless steel cookware set. Binoculars for older children, and—surprisingly to me, since music doesn't usually play a large part in the Amish lifestyle—several styles of well-made Hohner's harmonicas. Little red wagons, and an Amish-made adult-size old-fashioned scooter one can purchase in blue, red, lavender, dark green, hunter green, maroon, or navy (with the admonition that if no color is selected, they'll select one for you).

There are plenty of games, but no playing cards. Presumably playing cards are forbidden—as they were many years ago in most conservative churches—with or without gambling involved. There is a wooden, handmade rubber-band gun but nothing that resembles a real gun in any way. No cops and robbers. No cowboys and Indians—although there is a bow and arrow set with three suction-cupped, rubber-tipped arrows. No GI-Joe-type characters. No space aliens.

The thing that stands out to me about these toys isn't just the old-fashioned nature of this catalog, nor the fact that all of the toys have stood the test of time, nor the fact that none of them requires batteries, and that all require the child's participation. The thing that is *most* interesting to me is that, to my knowledge, none of them has been advertised on television in this decade.

Noticeably missing are any type of video games or technologically sophisticated toys.

I call her back to thank her for the catalog pages. "Amish children would be truly happy with just one or two of these gifts for Christmas?"

"Of course." Her voice is matter-of-fact. "Why wouldn't they be?"

And that describes Naomi and Luke's family Christmas. Why wouldn't the children be happy? After all, they'd each gotten a gift or two, the family had a nice meal, and they had fun with a makeshift toboggan with couch cushions on it.

I can't help but think that part of Naomi's children's satisfaction in their old-fashioned gifts might be that Amish children naturally have fewer wants without television commercials creating artificial standards by showing them what toys they should desperately need in order to be happy. Not to mention the television shows that portray huge piles of gifts beneath any family Christmas tree shown.

Their children also aren't spending time in the homes of other children who possess all the latest gizmos. This is one of the places where I think the uniformity of the Amish people really pays off. There is little reason for envy or jealousy on the part of the children because play things and possessions are basically the same in nearly all the Amish homes they visit.

This makes me ponder the number of gifts a child truly needs. I once read an essay by a woman who had taken the time to observe her small children's level of happiness with the gifts they opened at Christmas. After they had opened the first gift, they wanted to stop and play with it. But they couldn't play because they were made to wait until they had opened another gift. They were excited about the second gift and wanted to play with it, too, but there were grandparents and aunts and uncles giving them presents and there were many more gifts to unwrap, so she stopped them from playing with the first two gifts so they could open the third, and fourth, and so on, until the children were tired and overwhelmed, and instead of showing gratitude, they had begun to whine.

It was her opinion that small children are wired for no more than three gifts before the saturation point of excitement and happiness is reached and the crush of gifts becomes more than they can gracefully handle at one time.

This was just one mother's observations, not a scientific study, but it might be an interesting thing to observe with one's own children—to look for that point where the "wow" factor diminishes and the crankiness begins.

I find myself a little envious of Naomi's simple holiday. How easy such a Christmas must be. It seems too easy. Yet the satisfaction I read in her letter and voice seems as great as, if not greater than, my own.

Making Choices

"I grew tired of watching young actors roll their
eyes as though their parents were idiots."
—ENGLISCH MOTHER EXPLAINING WHY SHE ELIMINATED TELEVISION

I've been pretty negative about television, computers, cell phones, and social media in the writing of this book—and with good reason. They can be incredibly destructive.

On the other hand, these technological advances also have amazing, positive aspects. There are shows on television that are so well done that they can permanently change a life for the better or enrich a person's knowledge of the natural world. To a fragile elderly person living alone, television can be a great comfort. Ebook devices are making it possible for those with poor vision to read books. There are people I personally know in Hollywood who are devoting their lives to making movies that encourage and inspire. Computers can bring far-flung families back together and keep them closer. Cell phones can save a life or send an instant picture of a precious grandbaby across the country. Online shopping can be a boon to a shut-in or save hours of going from store to store for a busy parent on lunch break.

And technology can also help us *control* these very devices to which we can become addicted. There are filters for protecting ourselves and our children from inappropriate material on our computers. Just as important as locking one's door at night against intruders, these filters and controls need to be installed. There are programs that can also track one's computer time and present you with a detailed report of how you are spending it. I was recently having a conversation with a PR representative at one of the publishing houses I work for and this topic came up. She happened to be a young mother who was also making decisions on how to deal with technology and her family.

"People often compliment my husband and me on the behavior of our children," she said. "I'm not sure what we are doing right, except that we eliminated television from our lives. The more I watched, the more unhappy I became. Even the Disney Channel was a problem to me. If you watch, there is a certain built-in disrespect of parents in many of those programs. I grew tired of watching the young actors rolling their eyes as though their parents were idiots. I'm sure that is a major factor in the disrespect many parents experience with their children, and yet they probably think they are parenting well because they are allowing their children to only watch what is billed as 'family-friendly' programming."

Several families I know with young children don't exactly "have" television, but they do have a television set through which they, like Naomi, allow their children to occasionally watch some enjoyable but parent-chosen DVD.

These parents, like the Amish, are making deliberate, intentional choices about how they will use technology instead of allowing their families to be victims of it. It is not the easiest route for them to take, but I think it will pay dividends for them in the future.

Someone recently gave Leah's littlest boy, who is ten, a handheld, battery-operated video game. It feels strange to see a small Amish boy bent over a handheld video game, his thumbs flying with as much expertise as a non-Amish child.

It is a mixed blessing, and Leah is worried. On the one hand, she says it keeps him occupied on dark, winter days when he can't go outside, and battery-powered devices are not forbidden in her church. On the other hand, he'll play it incessantly, without stopping, unless she makes him put it down. This concerns her. Is she allowing too much of the world to creep into her home by allowing him to own this device?

Probably, is what I would like to say, but I don't weigh in on this topic. My role is to care about my friends, not attempt to advise them as they try to sort out how much modernity to allow in their lives. She's the mother and will have to make that decision, just as all the rest of us have had to make our decisions one by one on how much technology to allow our children to use and how much to allow ourselves to use as well.

It is easy, as a parent, to become discouraged. There is a lot of nasty stuff out there and it seems like it could pounce on our children and our families at any moment. Sometimes we forget that we are still in control. We are the ones who make the purchases and we are the ones who can control what we choose to do with those purchases.

A wonderful example of this went viral online recently. It was an iPhone "contract" from a mom, Janell Burley Hofmann, to her thirteen-year-old son in which she laid out the rules for his possession of an iPhone. In the contract she pointed out that she loved him, supported him, and was always in his corner, but that she also owned the cell phone, paid for the cell service, and would have the password to it at all times. She explained the reasoning behind her rules, and exactly what he could expect if the rules were not obeyed. The contract was humorous, warm, and engaging, but there was real steel behind that mother's words. It was obvious she was absolutely determined to protect her son from his own teenage stupidity, and I felt like giving her a standing ovation when I finished reading it.

Intentional, deliberate parenting that mirrors the Amish model—regardless of the issue—is parenting that has no interest in being liked by one's child or making that child "happy" and everything to do with protecting the child and the family. It takes a strong person to make hard, unpopular decisions, but that's part of the job. Anything less leaves our families unprotected and vulnerable.

Amish Parenting Tips
for the Non-Amish

- Life is short. Time with your children while they are still in your home is even shorter. Choose to take charge of this time and not let it evaporate on social media and internet surfing. Buy a timer and use it if you have to, or invest in a program that lets you know when you're nearing the time you have designated. Only allow yourself to spend that amount of time you've allotted yourself and no more.

- Try to intentionally turn off all electronic devices and television for everyone in the family for one evening per week. It probably won't feel at all natural. It might even feel awkward and uncomfortable. It will be especially challenging to bring this about in a household with older children who are used to near-constant cell phone connection to their friends. Do it anyway. This is important.

- Nothing in your life is as important as paying serious attention to your child. If you find yourself ignoring your child because you are texting or surfing the internet—you have a serious problem . . . and so will they. Decide how long you can safely spend on these activities without cutting into time your spouse and children need—and then stick to that limit. For instance, as a writer, research is part of my job. I need access to the internet to do some of it. I seldom have small children needing my attention anymore, but I still limit my access to the net by programming my computer to automatically shut off access for several hours each day. If I were more disciplined, I would not have to do this—but I'm not. I need artificial guardrails and this method helps me.

- Seriously consider dialing down the birthday and Christmas gifts. Your kids don't need another piece of plastic junk cluttering up their rooms. You don't need it cluttering up your credit card. Reward them with unhurried time with you instead.

- Have the courage to allow your child to experience a little boredom from time to time. Then let them use their own creativity to amuse themselves. Try to create some "white space" in a child's life instead of attempting to fill every minute.

· VI ·

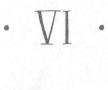

Faith

Faith

"I give thanks for all things."
—AMISH FATHER OF NINE

Between raising our family and being with the people who have made up the churches we've served, there are few life experiences my husband and I have not been intimately involved with. He has always been a hands-on preacher—the kind who visited the hospitals and shut-ins as well as working hard to try to keep people and families from falling apart. Life can be very hard, and I've watched him try to absorb at least some of the emotional pain people have brought to him.

I've also watched him become more and more a man of prayer as he realized that he could not take care of everyone's needs, no matter how hard or how long he worked. Because of his work, we have spent most of our lives being intimately connected to a large network of good people—just like our Amish friends.

What we've seen over the years is that some people seem much better able to overcome emotional and physical challenges than others. Some are whipped by circumstances that sometimes seem almost laughable in comparison to what others are going through.

When our county in southern Ohio went through the devastating flood of 1997, we mobilized our church to help the local people as best we could. The damage was so extensive that even the Red Cross and FEMA were overwhelmed, and so we did what we could to at least take care of our own local people's needs. Our church gave sacrificially and the work we did went on for months. One of the first things we did was pass out emergency food boxes to those who had lost everything.

The food boxes, which included enough food for a family of four for a week, were packed by volunteers in a facility in Nashville and then trucked, by volunteer truck drivers, through the night to our church parking lot where our men and women who owned pickup trucks distributed them to everyone we could find who was in need. We also had teams going out to help muck out houses and anything else we could do to help.

It wasn't easy because our area has a lot of hollows and winding dirt roads and we had no way of knowing exactly where the needs were. We just did the best we could. It was satisfying work because the people we helped were grateful and appreciative.

Except for one able-bodied young man who had been overlooked. He showed up at my doorstep absolutely livid because the water had come into his trailer and we hadn't brought him anything. He demanded to know why. He said he had a *right* to the food boxes we were delivering and a right to receive anything else we were handing out.

I remember being exhausted to the point of tears from days of nonstop work, and I said something about how we were just a little church trying to help the best we could—we weren't some big government agency. He didn't calm down until I dragged a heavy food box to the door and gave it to him.

This was before the Amish people began to move into our area, but I know absolutely that had he been an Amish man, he would not have been at my doorstep demanding his rights. It would never occur to him that he had *rights*. If an Amish man had come to my door, it would have been to ask how he and his people could help . . . and, more than likely, he would have had a child or two with him so they could learn the importance of helping neighbors.

When the Amish are baptized, in addition to confessing their faith in Jesus, they will kneel and denounce three things: the world, the devil, and . . . self. A denunciation of "self" is a promise to rid oneself of pride and disobedience.

One minister described this as a "death" to self, and explained that "dead people don't have rights."

In other words, the Amish are hardwired by example and solemn vow to believe that even suffering can have purpose in the larger picture of God's will. This, again, is the concept of *gelassenheit*—or fully surrendering to God's will, even if it means suffering.

The belief in *gelassenheit* makes for a stoic and enduring people.

I wasn't aware of just how stoic the Amish could be until our friend Henry was diagnosed with throat cancer. We received a letter from him while he was undergoing treatment. He wrote:

I am staying here at the Best Western while doing Radiation at the Lutheran Hospital. I go in once a day, have had 12 now with 17 to go. Feel fine except a sore throat. Dr. said that is normal. When I asked him about my voice in the long term, he just said 'God only knows.' So I felt that was a good way to feel about it overall. I'm just glad God is in control of it all and will reveal his perfect will in due time.

Three months later, we received another letter. Henry said that his prognosis was very hopeful after all the radiation. The doctors believed they might have gotten all of the tumor, but they didn't yet know for sure.

Then he wrote something that I found quite inspiring . . . and typically Amish.

> *I thank God for my cancer. Not because I'm happy that I have it, but because it is a command for me to do so. 1 Thessalonians 5:18 says, "In everything give thanks: for this is the will of God in Christ Jesus concerning you."*
>
> *God doesn't say to give thanks only for the good things in our lives. He says to give thanks in ALL things, and so I give thanks daily not only for the good things in my life, but for the things that are hard to accept, like my throat cancer, and it helps me.*

I received this letter only two days after getting some devastating news about a loved one's health. I had tossed and turned and lost sleep for both nights, but after receiving Henry's letter, I took his commitment to obedience to heart. At least, I went through the motions of saying the words of thanksgiving. Instead of simply begging for healing, I took the time to give thanks for the bad news—even though it made no earthly sense to do so. That small act of obedience somehow lightened the emotional panic for that day and the next as I continued to give thanks for something that at first overwhelmed me with fear. With each

prayer of thanks, the worry and fear lessened and the thankful-
ness grew.

Gelassenheit. My Amish friends tell me that it means that God
has a plan. God is in control. We don't have to carry everything
around on our shoulders. Someone bigger than us is taking care of
us even when we don't understand.

One of the many scriptures upon which *gelassenheit* is
founded is I Peter 5:7: "Cast all your anxiety on him because he
cares for you."

An Amish grandmother tells me that she believes this is one
of the most important things she can think of when it comes to
raising happy and contented children. She believes that having
faith that someone bigger than all of us is taking care of us even
when we don't understand why things are happening leads to a
healing and comforting environment in which both children and
adults can thrive.

I realize that not everyone reading this will be on board with
the faith aspect of Amish parenting, but it is impossible to separate the two. The Amish simply would not be Amish were it not
for the tenets of their faith. As Paul Stutzman has pointed out to
me multiple times, Amish parenting is *not* a method, it is a way
of life. Right or wrong, that way of life is built on their reverence
for God, their interpretation of the Bible, and their attempt to
apply the scriptures to their lives. And no matter what one believes, I think there are things we can all learn—and apply to our
lives—about parenting by observing how faith guides everything
the Amish do.

One of the most fascinating things about the Amish is, in
spite of their strong beliefs, they do not attempt to cajole or force
anyone to accept their brand of Christianity. Except for teaching

their own children, most of them do not engage in any form of evangelism. By the same token, my observations about the impact of their faith on their children and marriages are not given with the intention to convert anyone to Amish beliefs, but simply to explain who they are and why that might lead to them having the results that they do.

The Discipline of Patience

"Amish children are so much more patient than non-Amish children."
—HOLMES COUNTY NURSE

Before we moved to Ohio, I spent five years working as a court reporter in Detroit in family court. I listened to parents fighting over child support, visitation, child custody, pet custody, money, faithlessness, houses, and every kind of possession imaginable. Once I remember listening to a husband and wife fight it out over who should foot the bill for the extravagant wedding they'd had the month before.

Our courtrooms were a cacophony of upset people, filled with family members shouting their opinions, weeping, accusing, and finger-pointing . . . and, regrettably, there were frequently children present. Usually the children were there because someone had to testify and didn't have a babysitter.

Shelley was one of the courts' permanent attorneys assigned to one of the judges. She was good at her job, partly because she was smart and experienced in the ways of family court, and partly because she was a large woman who was not easily intimidated by irate family members. She seemed to sail through her work with a great attitude and a smile on her face.

"Watch the children," she said to me one day during a break. "You can always tell which ones have been raised in church."

"How?"

"Churched children are the ones who have learned to sit still, who have learned to be patient."

I was intrigued. I knew she had evidence for what she was talking about. As a court attorney, one of Shelley's jobs was to interview the people in each case. She knew the backgrounds of the children in her cases, and sometimes church attendance—or lack of it—became part of the conversation.

"Just watch," Shelley said, as we went back into the courtroom. "You can always tell. Children who have been taken to church know how to behave."

I agree with Shelley up to a point.

Some children are just naturally more energetic than others. In our church there is one wing of our auditorium that we affectionately refer to as "the jungle" because that's where the parents of young children gravitate. They help one another pluck runaway toddlers out of the aisles, crawlers out from under the seats, retrieve dropped toys, and share Cheerios. Other parents are able to sit front and center with their perfectly obedient and quiet children. My husband tries to reassure harried young mothers that there isn't a baby in the world who can cry louder than he can preach, but sometimes this statement is put to the test—most recently by our own grandbaby.

I once asked an elementary schoolteacher who attends our church if she can tell a difference in behavior between churched and unchurched children.

"In general children who are taken to church are better be-haved," she said, "but there are exceptions."

I don't think my lawyer friend Shelley's litmus test is absolute, but I was reminded of her observation the first time I ever at-tended an Old Order Amish service, which was the same morn-ing I attended Rebecca's wedding.

Amish worship is not a hurried affair. As I sat there, I had plenty of time to observe the children, and what I saw was im-pressive. Even the smallest of toddlers seemed relatively content. One little girl played with her mother's handkerchief, quietly folding and unfolding it. Another small child ran a tiny tractor over a grandfather's knee. Another one peacefully munched on a cracker.

During worship, Amish men and women sat on opposite sides of the group, facing each other. One little boy tired of his mother's lap and wandered across the middle section of the barn from the women's side to the men's section, walking directly in front of the Amish minister who was preaching. The preacher didn't miss a beat as the child toddled past and clambered into his waiting father's arms.

Except for one moment, when a mother, tired of wrestling an active child about ten months old, walked over to the men's side and plopped him on his father's lap, as though to say, "Here, you take care of this child for a while," I saw no evidence of the frus-tration I'd often felt while trying to care for my own three boys as they squirmed on various church pews when they were small.

I have enormous sympathy and respect for young parents wrestling with children through church. It was not easy keeping my boys quiet during services—especially since my husband was usually in the pulpit and so I had to deal with them alone.

My biggest discipline problem was our middle son, Caleb. He was a charmer and knew it. As the minister's wife, I felt it was my duty to sit up front, but that only served to give Caleb an audience. He smiled, made faces, and practically danced on top of my head to amuse the people behind us.

One day, at age two, when he couldn't manage to attract the full attention of the woman behind us, he deliberately blew a handful of chewed-up graham crackers onto her well-tailored lap. She was the mother of one perfectly behaved little girl and had no sympathy for mothers of imperfect little boys. She brushed graham cracker crumbs off her skirt as I apologized, but the next Sunday I eliminated graham crackers from my repertoire of kid's church snacks and quietly moved to the other side of the auditorium.

I got through the hard years of getting children through worship the best I could. There were definitely many Sundays when I wondered why I even bothered to come at all when it seemed like all I accomplished was wrestling with my squirming boys, so it was interesting to me that even in an Amish church, some children *did* take a break and go outside. Older ones left to go to the bathroom alone and were gone just long enough that I suspected they might have lingered a bit on their way back in. Others helped themselves to water from the cooler set up in the back of the barn before rejoining a parent on the hard, backless benches.

"Were you surprised at how much our children move around?" my friend Naomi asked after the service.

"Maybe some," I admitted.

"Moving around a little helps them get through it," Naomi said. "They eventually grow out of the need and learn to sit still."

The Amish don't have a lot of bells and whistles in their church services. In fact, they don't have any. Their services are as plain as their clothing. They listen to preaching and to scripture being read. They pray. They sing.

Their songs come out of the *Ausbund*, the oldest continuously used hymn book in the world, and the songs are sung agonizingly slow. I recently found out that there is a good reason for the slow tempo of the songs: most of the hymns were written by martyrs waiting in prison for torture and death.

Like the apostles of the first century, Anabaptist martyrs sang hymns to encourage one another as they sat in prison around five hundred years ago. Some of the jailors started mocking their faith by dancing to the hymns the prisoners sang. The martyrs dealt with this mockery by deliberately slowing the hymns down until it was impossible to dance to them. That practice still exists today. Actually, they sing their hymns so slowly, there is an Amish joke that it is possible to arrive to church late, unhitch the horse, rub it down, give it feed, and still come in and get settled on a bench before the people have finished singing the first verse of the opening hymn.

This is, of course, an exaggeration, but not by much. The Amish hymns are sung a cappella with no harmony, no written melody, and no real rhythm. The songs are eerie and dirgelike to an unaccustomed Englisch ear. Most have multiple verses and they sing every last one.

In other words, if there is one thing the Amish don't do, it is rush through their church services. They don't seem to expect them to even be mildly entertaining. When they come to church, they patiently settle down for the duration. Like so much else in the Amish tradition, this is the way it always has been and probably always will be.

It takes patience to sit through three- to four-hour church services while sitting on hard, backless benches. It also takes patience to sing the slow, ancient hymns. The Amish are okay with that, though. They believe that children need to learn patience.

There is no Sunday school. There are no bulletins for the children to draw on or fold into an airplane to sail over an unsuspecting congregation's heads, as my youngest son managed to do one memorable Sunday. There is no children's worship, no puppets, or really anything at all to engage a child's attention.

The Amish greatly respect the biblical teachings about the "fruits of the spirit" mentioned in Galatians 5:22–23. One of those fruits comes from the Greek word *makrothumia*, which literally translates as "long-tempered." It is rendered in various English translations of the Bible as "patience," "long-suffering," or "forbearance."

Patience, long-suffering, and forbearance are built into the Amish psyche and lifestyle, not only in their church services, but in many other practical ways. It takes patience to plod along in a horse and buggy at ten miles per hour while Englisch cars whiz past. It takes patience to plow one's fields with teams of horses while a tractor-owning Englisch neighbor plows several fields in a fraction of the time. It takes patience to dress in such a way that makes tourists gawk and point. It takes patience to walk all the way out to the phone shanty every time one needs to make a phone call and patience to deal with the myriad of relatives who live close by.

But there are payoffs.

Patience pays off in the much-sought-after Amish-made items that sometimes support entire communities. Amish furniture, baskets, quilts, food, and sturdily built houses are renowned for excellent craftsmanship and quality. I was struck by the slow, deliberate pace of a small crew of Amish men whom we hired to build a barn behind our house. They took the time to do an excellent job. Nothing is done slapdash. These are not hurried people.

"Where the difference between Amish children and the non-Amish is really apparent," one nurse in Holmes County tells me, "is at the doctor or the dentist's office. Amish children are so much more patient than non-Amish children. They even seem less frightened and able to endure more pain. Of course," she muses, "so are their parents."

Patience is a virtue in the Amish culture, and learning to sit quietly during worship services is one of the places it is learned. Amish parents don't appear to be concerned if their child is bored with church, or bored, period.

That is seldom true with Englisch parents. We tend to worry if our children aren't well-stimulated and engaged in enjoyable or educational activities at all times. I watch loving parents scramble to create an almost constant stream of entertainment and activities for their children and I wonder if this is the wisest choice.

If one never has to sit still and engage one's mind as a child, if one is constantly being entertained, when does personal creativity develop? When does patience kick in? When does one ever develop the ability to wait?

At the church where my husband preaches, we try to make children feel welcome. I love watching them skip off to their Sunday school classes and listening to their squeals and giggles afterward as they climb all over the playground equipment outside.

We try not to make church a matter of endurance for our children, but they are expected to sit as quietly as possible through at least a portion of the worship service. I suspect that this regular time of prayer, singing, and teaching might have more of a positive effect on our children than we realize. Taking our children to church isn't always easy, but I believe if it is done on a consistent basis it can have a very positive effect on even the smallest children.

"This is important," the parent is saying by bringing their children to church. "It is only a small part of our week, but it is an important part. Here is a cracker to munch on. Now sit still and learn to pay attention. You are not the center of our universe. God is."

Fostering Forgiveness

"In the Amish culture, forgiveness is not a choice, but an expectation."
—PAUL STUTZMAN

In 2006, the world watched in awe as the Amish reached out in healing forgiveness to the family of the man who killed five Amish girls in the Nickel Mines schoolhouse tragedy.

In an interview that was conducted later with the killer's mother, she described how her husband was so broken by his son's behavior that he quite literally could not hold his head up . . . until members of the Amish community came and put their arms around him in forgiveness. In a world torn with hate and anger, we all watched the Amish make a deliberate, intentional choice to forgive the killer, reach out to his family, and begin the healing of a community.

This did not follow the script that people who are not familiar with the Amish culture would have predicted. Rage, anger, despair, vindictiveness, lawsuits, recriminations . . . that is what most people would expect as a natural and very human reaction.

Those of us familiar with how strongly the Amish feel about

forgiveness were impressed, but we were not surprised by what we saw. We watched the Amish go about their lives deliberately trying to bring about what healing they could by doing exactly what they've always done—practicing forgiveness.

In the same way that the Amish believe in showing love through actions rather than words, they forgave the murderer, not by words alone, but by deliberately and immediately reaching out to his family.

I guarantee that all the Amish surrounding the Nickel Mines tragedy would have been grateful if the crush of newspeople had never arrived. They did not ask for nor want the publicity that came after the event, but to the best of their ability they responded to the questions and photos thrust upon them with faith and forgiveness even as they grieved.

My friend Katie, an Old Order Amish woman from Michigan, was in the Nickel Mines area for a family wedding when this terrible thing happened. Her daughter, an Amish schoolteacher, became quite emotional when she heard what had happened, especially when she heard about the young schoolteacher who offered to be killed instead of the children. Together, Katie and her daughter and another relative went to the schoolhouse.

"We just wanted to go there and pray," Katie told me. "I did not realize there would be so many newspeople there. The police were blocking everyone from going to the school, but when they saw us, they let us through. We stood at the fence near the school and prayed and cried. When we tried to go back, the newspeople insisted on talking to us. I was really nervous, so I prayed for words and for courage. It was very hard to face all those people."

Katie is a small woman with a quiet voice who has lived a quiet life. She was in her late fifties when the tragedy occurred and was quite possibly the last person I would expect to be able to speak up while surrounded by cameras and microphones. The Amish people grow up avoiding cameras the best they can, but suddenly, for Katie, cameras were unavoidable.

There are two pictures I later found in some newspapers. One is of Katie standing at the fence with her daughter and another relative. There is a terrible look of grief on the face of the three women. The second one shows Katie being interviewed by Ann Curry. The space surrounding Katie and the newswoman is bristling with microphones and cameras. She looks small and vulnerable in her white *kapp* and plain clothes, suddenly thrust into the limelight.

The Amish are so closely knit together that sometimes I think they don't feel things solely as individuals; they feel things as a community. When one has good news, they are all happy. When one is experiencing sorrow, all experience sorrow.

And yet, in spite of her broken heart, Katie answered the questions, and spoke about her faith and forgiveness with quiet courage.

"God gave me the words," she told me, "although I was so nervous I can't exactly remember what I said."

I looked online again to find out what words Katie had used. This is what she said: "You see, at a very young age our parents teach us to forgive like Christ did, but not man-made forgiveness. Jesus still takes care of us, even if bad things happen. These children are in Heaven. We still weep and cry just like everyone else, but then we go to Christ. We are really strongly taught to forgive like Jesus did. We forgive the way Christ forgives us."

It was a stunning example of the deliberate application of passages like Matthew 6:14–15: "For if you forgive other people when they sin against you, your heavenly Father will also forgive you. But if you do not forgive others their sins, your Father will not forgive your sins."

Katie's words, along with those of other Amish who were interviewed during the harrowing days following the tragedy, were trumpeted around the globe to a world shocked into awe over the Amish culture's determination to forgive.

Forgiveness, to the Amish, is not an accident, nor even an individual choice. The best way I can describe it is that they intentionally *nurture* a culture of forgiveness. This attitude, like so much else in their culture, goes back hundreds of years to their martyrs.

The *Martyrs Mirror* is a one-thousand-page book that has helped define the Amish and Mennonite people. It was written specifically about the Anabaptist martyrs. *Anabaptist* means "second baptizers." By the 1500s, infant baptism was the norm in the established church. Then Martin Luther upset the religious applecart in 1534 by translating the Bible from the original Hebrew, Aramaic, and Greek into the common language of the German people. The printing press had been invented by then, and suddenly the Bible was affordable and available even to shopkeepers and housewives. People started reading it for themselves and it was as though a light had been turned on. No longer did the people have to rely on clergymen to tell them what the Bible said; they could read it for themselves. One of the first things they noticed was that the practice of infant baptism was not recorded in the pages of the Bible.

Those adults who had been baptized as infants began to choose to be baptized a second time. This did not sit well with the established church leaders, who began to hunt down and kill Anabaptists for not upholding the status quo. This was relatively easy to do because the Anabaptists believed equally strongly in the doctrine of nonresistance. In other words, they could hide, but they could not put up any self-defense. Suddenly, it was open season on those who defied church doctrine.

One of the most famous stories within the *Martyrs Mirror* involves an Anabaptist martyr named Dirk Willems, who managed to escape his prison cell by climbing out of the window on a rope made of rags. He ran but was seen by a guard who gave chase. Dirk, because of his lighter weight resulting from prison starvation, was able to run across a frozen body of water; his pursuer, who was heavier, fell through. The pursuer begged for help, and Dirk, instead of continuing to run, turned around and saved the man's life. His kindness was rewarded by being reimprisoned, tortured, and eventually burned at the stake.

This story, in the minds of the Amish, represents the epitome of Christlike behavior and nonresistance. Escape would have been fine for Dirk, but to have allowed the guard to drown would have been unthinkable.

It would be unusual to find an Amish home that does not have the thick volume of the *Martyrs Mirror* on their bookshelf. Many Amish parents, who normally shield their children from any hint of violence, place their children on their knee and read to them out of this book. The stories are passed down through the generations. It is a part of every Amish person's psyche. This is who we are, the book tells them. This is what we did. These are the courageous and faithful people from whom we come.

Recently, a young Amish woman from Holmes County wrote a children's version of the *Martyrs Mirror* and illustrated it. From what I hear, the book is selling well. I sat beside her at a book signing and she told me that she had written and illustrated it primarily to keep the stories alive and in the children's minds—while taking a little of the gruesomeness out of the ancient woodcut illustrations.

The value to their culture of imprinting this special identity upon the children cannot be underestimated. When one is meeting and chatting with Amish people, it is easy to be lulled into a feeling of familiarity. They cook meals, we cook meals. They love their children, we love our children. They work hard to pay their bills, we work hard to pay our bills.

The thing most outsiders underestimate is that the blood of martyrs runs not only in the veins of these people, but through their consciousness as well.

If Jesus Christ could forgive and ask his father to forgive his torturers, then they can forgive one another. If Dirk Willems was able to forgive his prison guard long enough to save him from the frozen waters at the cost of his own life, they can forgive their neighbor a cow that wanders through a fence, or they can forgive a husband who tracks mud into a clean house.

Children see this culture of forgiveness modeled most forcefully within the church when confessions are made. There is nothing that cannot be forgiven as long as the person asking for forgiveness truly turns away from sinful ways.

Nurturing a culture of forgiveness has an effect on absolutely everything—relationships within a church, relationships within a marriage, relationships between parents and children, between siblings and cousins.

To live with such interconnectedness and such constant fellowship takes a lot of forgiveness. The ability to forgive is a major factor in the Amish church's ability to survive and thrive for five centuries.

Teaching Generosity

"Children need to see a sermon instead of hearing one."
—OLD ORDER DEACON

The need to be a good example rather than telling children how they should behave was stated over and over as I went about asking the Amish for advice on how to raise children. As they try to model good behavior in front of their children, the Amish take to heart I Corinthians 11:1: "Follow my example, as I follow the example of Christ."

"Children learn about giving to others by helping a parent take meals to a neighbor, and sometimes those children learn by seeing a neighbor bring meals to *them* when something bad has happened in their family," an Amish grandmother told me.

"I remember when I was a teenager," an Amish man said, "I had a cousin who would come to our house and write a check. My father would then 'cash' it for him. The cousin was going through a hard time financially. Sometimes his checks weren't any good and my father *knew* the check might not be good, but he cashed them all the same and never said a word if they were bad. I asked him why he put up with it and he said it was because my cousin needed the money and he had a little extra that he could afford to share. My father's quiet kindness made quite an impression on me."

Luke told me another story. "It seemed as though my father was constantly taking me along with him to various neighbors who needed help. If the neighbor was ill, we'd go and plow or harvest or do any number of things to help out. If the woman was ill, my mother would take me along to help her clean or carry food. Not only did it teach me that I should help others, it made me feel a lot more secure as a child. I saw this behavior so consistently out of my people that I knew if my family ever fell on hard times, help would be available. It's one of the reasons I've always loved our culture—this belief in helping."

As I hear these words and evaluate the impact that seeing these sorts of actions might have on children, I'm immediately reminded of a time in our family's life when we lived in Detroit. I became quite ill and my husband had to rush me to the hospital. Before we left our house, my husband called one of the women from our church to come and care for our eight-year-old son.

Many years later, our family was talking about that incident and my son told me that the kindness he received from Mrs. Betty Patton that day had a profound and lasting effect upon his attitude about our church.

"You'd not been feeling well for several days, Mom," he recounts now. "When Dad drove away with you, I was really scared. Then Mrs. Patton came and she washed the dishes, and fixed me food, and told me that everything would be okay, and I believed her. She was so kind. As a child, it was such a relief to know that someone was taking care of me even though you and Dad couldn't be there."

An Amish mother explained her people's philosophy to me. "We spend a lot of time trying to teach our children the Golden Rule—to do unto others as you would have others do unto you— by our own example in how we treat others."

An Amish deacon said, "If I cheat someone in business, my son will see and become a cheater. If I am honest, there is a much greater chance that my son will grow up to be an honest man as well. There are many things I've done, not just because they are the right things to do, but because I know my children are watching and learning with every move I make."

Lester told me something interesting about being an example when I was interviewing him and the other men at Keim Lumber. He said that as an imperfect leader of his family, he especially appreciates forgiveness. That he makes mistakes and hopes that his family will forgive him when he is wrong, but that he also tries to model forgiveness in front of his wife and children.

"For instance," he says, "if a neighbor behaves badly, I try to teach my children to forgive that neighbor by actively forgiving the neighbor myself."

Many Englisch children who are part of a church are handed a quarter or a dollar to put in the collection plate as it is passed in front of them. Well-meaning parents use this as a way to teach children the necessity and self-discipline of giving or tithing.

This is not usually the Amish way. In fact, when I questioned Luke about how they went about tithing, he looked a little confused. The collection plate is not regularly passed during Amish worship. Nor are families (and children) expected to "tithe," since it is not an actual command within the New Testament (tithing is part of the Old Testament teaching), so they consider it not to apply to them. In some ways, however, they hold themselves to a higher responsibility.

"A tenth of our income?" Luke mused over the thought. "We just give as we are able when there is a need. Sometimes it might be a tenth, sometimes less, sometimes a lot more. It depends on what we have, and how great the need is."

I tried to wrap my mind around this. They just give whenever and whatever? How does the church function?

"Well, our church doesn't have the expenses that yours probably does," he said. "Our ministers and bishops just serve . . . they don't get paid. And we don't have church buildings to keep up because we use our own homes to worship in. No utilities on church buildings. No taxes." He shrugged apologetically. He did not want to make it seem as though he was criticizing the way we do things.

He was especially careful with his words because he was aware that my husband is paid to be a full-time minister, and we do have a church building with upkeep and utilities that require weekly contributions. We also have a budget for a great deal of what we term benevolent work, both in our community and internationally.

Sometimes the burden of keeping up with all the requests for money becomes nearly overwhelming to our church leaders. There are near-constant phone calls from people asking for help with utilities, gasoline, food, mortgage payments, or even diapers, often from people we've never seen nor heard of. It is hard to know what to do and whom to help.

"So what does the money you do contribute go toward?" I asked.

"Taking care of our own people," he said. "If there are widows or fatherless children within our own church, they are cared for first. There is help with medical bills as well when necessary."

The Amish adhere to the teaching in Galatians 6:10: "As we have opportunity therefore let us do good unto all men, but especially those of the household of faith."

Luke's description of the way his church deals with finances is so typically Amish. Families aren't expected to give more than they are able, and people from within their own church are cared for first.

Their children are not handed money from a parent's pocket in an attempt to train them to give. That money has cost the child nothing, and so it teaches little. The children, not yet old enough to become members of the church, are not expected to help shoulder the financial costs inherent in being a member.

I once knew a very openly religious Englisch parent who boasted that he didn't allow his young daughters to just give ten percent of their babysitting money to the church, he required them to give *twenty* percent. I knew these girls and was aware of the enormous resentment that bubbled within them over that and other religious observations that seemed to have more to do with their father's pride than with actual scripture. Things did not turn out well for that family.

Amish children, on the other hand, might see their parents looking over their finances while discussing how much they can spare to help someone specific who is in need. Often they see parents choosing to share their money sacrificially in order to help out an Amish brother or sister. They see parents shouldering the responsibility of aging parents. They see mothers and fathers sometimes doing without in order to help a neighbor.

Giving, in the Amish way of thinking, is not just about

money. If a barn burns, the Amish community comes together to help the family rebuild. If a house is destroyed by fire or a flood, the Amish community will be there. They will donate expertise, hours of work, and sometimes equipment and supplies.

Even in small ways they are givers. It is unusual, when I am visiting with Amish friends, to come away from their homes without a small gift of some kind. A jar of preserves, homemade pickles, some applesauce, a loaf of homemade bread, a potted flower, special seeds—and always a patient and generous dose of knowledge and friendship. Giving is deeply ingrained in the Amish spirit. I believe most Amish children see evidence of various kinds of giving on an almost daily basis. Because of this, they learn to be givers by example, not just words.

One does not have to be Amish in order to teach children to be generous.

We knew an Englisch couple who were far from rich. The father had a decent job and both he and his wife were frugal people. Each Sunday, they gave a certain set percentage of their income to their church, but they also put a percentage into a bank account that was an emergency fund their family used for addressing other people's needs. If one of their children, for instance, was worried about a child in their class who needed a warm coat or school supplies, the mother would purchase those items and quietly give them to the teacher to be given anonymously to the needy child. When a woman who had been attending our church got the courage to leave an abusive husband, this family financed her move and paid for the first month's rent on her new apartment. They decided these things only after a meeting, where all five family members voted. The mother and father seriously weighed their children's viewpoints on every situation.

This emergency fund was a closely guarded family secret that they told no one, except their minister, my husband, so he would be able to come to them if there was a need within the church that they might address. Those secret meetings they held to discuss helping other people did something special to that family. Those three children are grown up now and all are quite successful—and they are also three of the most caring and responsible adults I've ever known. Still in their twenties, they have already done more good than some people do in a lifetime.

Choosing Your Faith

"I'm leaving."
—AMISH GIRL

"Tell me something," a friend from my church said as he stopped me in the foyer of our church building soon after my first visit to Amish country. "How can Amish parents justify telling their teenagers to go out and do whatever they want once they turn sixteen? How can a parent do that?"

This was a loving father and grandfather. His question was sincere.

"What makes you think that happens?" I asked.

"There was this program on TV that said that during something I think they call rumspringa, Amish kids are allowed to do whatever they want to do and their parents just sit around hoping they'll eventually come back to their church."

After watching some so-called documentaries, I have to admit, that had been my impression as well. That was before I actually got to know several Amish parents who were raising teenagers. Rumspringa looms large in the Englisch view of Amish life, and television shows and movies that depict Amish teenagers drinking, doing drugs, smoking, and having wild sexual encounters have taken root in the American consciousness.

From the time Amish children turn sixteen, they have to wrestle with the decision of whether or not to accept the faith of their parents and community. It is not a decision easily made, and the ramifications either way are enormous. During this period of decision forming, they are allowed to experience many of the things forbidden in the church, and many of them do get things like iPhones or driver's licenses. But the TV shows and movies have not always given an accurate depiction of what rumspringa is really like. This is meant to be a time where children are allowed to decide whether or not the Amish life—and the Amish faith—is for them.

If, at the end of their rumspringa, a person chooses to become Englisch instead of being baptized into the Amish church, he or she will be allowed to leave the community. They will still be allowed to have some fellowship with their Amish family, but they will not live within the community, and the relationships are never quite as tight-knit from that point on.

However, if a young person decides to stay Amish, they must stand by that choice. After enjoying a few years of driver's licenses, cars, radios, cell phones, Englisch dress, movies, the internet, and even the freedom to pursue more education, an Amish youth has to face—if he or she is going to remain Amish—putting all that away, selling the car, climbing into a buggy, dressing plainly for the rest of their life—and presumably never look back.

Once a young person is baptized into the Amish church, they cannot leave it without the possibility of being shunned. This ban, or shunning, is stricter in some sects than others, but the possibility is always there.

In other words, becoming Amish is not a superficial choice that one can wander in and out of. It is a deadly serious commitment and one that no Amish person takes lightly.

To make sure they know what they're getting into, teenagers are given a bit more freedom to find out about the outside world. "It isn't that we allow them to just go out and go crazy," Mary tells me. "They are given more freedom, yes, just like your Englisch teenagers are given when they are old enough to drive. But we worry and pray, just like you, that they'll stay away from alcohol and drugs. It isn't as though we push them through the door and tell them to go be as sinful as they can be."

I'm no expert on Amish teens, but when I see them, they are usually working: Naomi's girls, washing dishes, doing chores, going to their outside jobs, cooking, sewing, bringing home their paychecks. Mary's sons, going off to their jobs as carpenters before daybreak and working hard around the family farm in what spare time they have in the evenings. These are not the out-of-control teenagers you see on some of the television shows. These are polite, reasonably contented kids who are hardworking, respectful to their parents, and kind to one another. This is the reality I see.

So, in order to talk about Amish teenagers for this book, I turned to Paul, the expert, who ran with Amish boys during his Mennonite youth.

"Tell me everything you know about rumspringa," I said.

We were sitting in the Victorian front parlor of the Hotel Millersburg with a pot of coffee between us. This was where we pounded out most of the plans for this book, and we were no longer a curiosity to the staff, as we sat there with our computers and notebooks and stacks of notecards.

Paul took a sip of coffee, then carefully set it back down and stared at the table without answering. I assumed he was simply taking the time to gather his thoughts. Paul has been an easy co-author with whom to work. We'd been able to weigh and discard various ideas about this book without either of us taking offense. If anything, I'd had to caution him, with his pacifist Mennonite background, from being too nice to contradict me. I didn't want a coauthor who agreed with everything I said.

Therefore, I am surprised by the anger that flashes in his eyes when he finally looks up at me.

"Whoa," I said. "Did I say something wrong?"

"No," Paul answered. "It's just that I despise the word *rums-pringa.*"

I was caught completely off-guard. "What is wrong with the word *rumspringa*?"

"It is a term that was coined by the media for exploitive pur-poses," he said. "The Englisch media has given non-Amish peo-ple the idea that at age sixteen, Amish parents basically throw up their hands and give their children permission to do whatever they want whenever they want to do it with the idea that when they do come back to the church, they will have gotten worldli-ness out of their system."

I admitted that was pretty much the impression I had before I actually knew the Amish.

"You and your husband are part of a conservative church, Serena," he said. "When you were raising your sons and they turned sixteen, did you throw in the towel and let them do what-ever they wanted?"

"Of course not," I said. "They had curfews. We expected to know where they were, what they were doing, and who they were with. We tried to give them enough freedom to grow up, but they knew we'd be paying attention and would put up some barriers if we saw them abusing their freedom."

"Exactly," Paul said. "That's what my wife and I did with our children. That's what most Amish parents do as well."

"Then how did the idea of rumspringa being a deliberately wild and crazy time get started?"

"*Rumspringa* simply means 'running around,'" Paul said. "If you went to an Amish friend's house and asked where one of their teenage children were, the parent might say, 'Oh, he's out running around.' Those few years after age sixteen, before one formally joins the church, are an especially social time for young people. They go to one another's homes, attend singings, play games, and check out other youth from other Amish churches. It is primarily a time for finding someone to marry."

"So you're saying the drunken barn parties are a myth?"

"No." Paul shook his head. "They happen—but they certainly aren't condoned by the church, and not all Amish kids participate. My experience is that the large percentage of Amish teens don't really step all that far outside the lines of how they were raised. They might cut their hair and buy some Englisch clothes for a while. Many get driver's licenses and carry cell phones. Most of them are too busy working a full-time job to get into much trouble at all. The main thing I want people to realize is that Amish parents aren't pushing their teenagers to go out and experience every possible vice just so they'll get it out of their systems. That would be foolish, and the Amish are not a foolish people."

A few weeks later, I dropped in and found Naomi and a younger daughter cleaning out the upper section of their barn. The barn is huge, and practically empty. A dairy business had been tried and abandoned. The only thing the barn is used for now is housing one cow that provides milk for the family's needs, a multiplicity of barn cats, and the family dogs.

While Naomi and I talked, the younger daughter became bored and asked permission to go back to the house. Naomi surprised me by letting her daughter go before the work was finished. The minute the girl was gone, I realized why. My friend had bad news and wanted privacy to talk to me about it.

A light rain had begun to fall and the sound of rain on the tin roof made the top story of the barn feel comfortable and cozy. I spent a great deal of my childhood playing in barns much like this one. The smell of hay and the sounds of pigeons roosting in the rafters brought back good memories, and yet there was a feeling of dread in the pit of my stomach. I was afraid I knew what Naomi wanted to talk with me about.

"Have a seat." She arranged two stray bales of hay close together to create a comfortable place for us to sit while we talked.

"Fanny is leaving," Naomi told me. "She's leaving the Amish church."

I closed my eyes, absorbing the impact of this statement. I love this family and am impressed with the life these parents have given their children. To so many people, the life this girl has lived would seem ideal. In my eyes, she has had all the love and nurturing a daughter could possibly want.

But I had been seeing the signs. Her "running around" period had lasted longer than most. She was of marrying age and there was as of yet no young man asking her to marry. For several years she had worn only a small, black, lace head covering instead of the white prayer *kapp* of her mother and younger sisters. She owned a car, used an iPhone, and had a job in which she "worked out."

"I'm so sorry, Naomi."

I waited for tears. For anger. For hurt to show in Naomi's face. I knew how deeply she valued the heritage she had been raised with and tries to preserve within her family.

"Are you okay?" I asked.

"I am," Naomi assured me. "My husband and I have done our job. We have taught her well. She knows the Lord. She values the scriptures. She is a grown woman and it is time for her to make her own decisions. I have peace that she will make good ones."

There was a stoic acceptance in Naomi's voice. I was astonished and impressed. Fanny was leaving the church of her forebears and Naomi was at peace?

I did not know if this behavior was typical or not. I'd never been through this before.

A few days later, I found myself alone with Fanny for a few minutes.

"I hear you've made a big decision," I said.

"Yes," she said, "I'm leaving."

"It really isn't greener on the other side of the fence, you know," I said, thinking of all the people I know who wish they could have been raised in such a nurturing environment. "You might be losing a whole lot more than you realize if you go through with this."

"I know what I'm doing," she told me.

"Where will you go?"

She looked around at the big, old, honest house where she and her siblings had grown up. "I think they'll allow me to stay here for a while. I have not been baptized into the Amish church yet, so I can't be shunned, but I'm not sure what to expect."

I didn't know, either. Her parents are kind and compassionate people, but the church and their family is their life. In spite of Naomi's acceptance, I know this daughter's decision had to have been difficult.

"When you have a family of your own," I said awkwardly, "you will be giving up much that is good for your family. Are you sure having electricity and a car is worth it?"

In my opinion, this girl was taking a huge risk.

"I'm not leaving because I want to have electricity in my life," Fanny said. "I'm leaving because I want more spirituality in my life. I've found a church that I really like."

"What kind of a church?"

"We don't really have a name. We're not very big. Just a few of us who study the Bible together. I've learned so much."

"What do they teach?"

"The Bible." She smiled. "And they have a band!"

"A band?"

"One of the girls I've become friends with in the church plays guitar."

I knew that Fanny also played guitar and wrote songs. Now that she had an outlet for her music, I doubted that she'd be coming back to the Amish church anytime soon.

A couple months later, I saw Fanny again. She had not wavered in her newfound freedom. She was wearing blue jeans and her hair was down. She looked stunning, as well as happy.

"I realize that driving a car or having electricity will not necessarily send a person to hell," Naomi told me later. "But I also know it is possible to lose our culture entirely within one generation. I would hate to see that happen. I believe the life we have is a good and rare thing."

And yet, the Amish still let their children choose.

Why? Because in spite of all the teaching they give their children, in spite of all the prayers, and all the church services, they do not believe it is possible to inherit or impose faith. Each individual must choose. This freedom to choose is rooted in the very beginnings of the Anabaptist movement. Five hundred years ago, they rejected the practice of infant baptism because they believed becoming a Christian had to be an individual decision and commitment. They have not changed in that belief.

What We Can Learn

"Why do these people keep coming here?"
—A MENNONITE PUZZLING OVER TOURISTS

A frequent topic of conversation among those who live and work in the Holmes County area is the fact that more than three million tourists visit "Amish country" every year. That figure has grown to the point that I feel sorry for the Amish people as they contend with the congested traffic and avid curiosity of so many tourists.

Not that the Amish mind the business that tourism brings in. On the whole they speak well of the visitors who come to their area, but most can remember a time when it was much safer to travel by buggy or bicycle than it is now.

I frequently ask both Amish and non-Amish residents in this area what they think the big draw is. Why, in their opinion, has this area become the biggest tourist attraction in the state of Ohio?

A Mennonite business owner who has spent his entire life within a few miles of the heart of Amish country discussed that very question with me recently.

"They come here by the millions," the business owner said.

"And what for? To watch a horse take a dump in the middle of the road? To see a woman walk around in a long dress and bonnet? To watch corn grow? To eat cheese? It's not like this place is Disneyland or anything."

"Maybe it's for the pie," I joked, but he didn't laugh.

"I'll tell you why they come, and it isn't just to eat homemade pie."

"Tell me." I really wanted to hear his answer.

"The older people come because they see things that they remember from their childhoods—so they come for the nostalgia. They enjoy seeing things like a man plowing a field with a team of horses. It makes them feel safe. But those who are a bit younger, now, that's where it gets interesting."

"Why do you think the younger people come?" I asked.

"For the same reasons that they read your novels about the Amish," he answered. "The reasons they watch old reruns of *The Waltons*, or *Little House on the Prairie*. They're looking for decency, for simplicity, for goodness. They want to feel safe again. There is a great hunger in our country to be around people who actually stand for something. So tourists come here to watch a people sacrificing modern conveniences because of their faith, and it makes them feel a little better about life in general."

"I think you might be right about that," I agreed.

"The bottom line, in my estimation, is that they come here because they are hungry for God, and for people who are living godly lives. They don't realize it, of course, but I think that's really at the root of why they come."

Many mainstream Christian churches are shrinking. Church leaders scramble to find new ways to bring people through the doors. Various evangelistic fads come and go. I read an article recently on why some churches are losing so many who were raised in church. The author's hypothesis was that basically we have become irrelevant in our worship services. He said that this postmodern generation, raised on movies and videos, requires—at the very least—solid PowerPoint illustrations, great (and short) sermons, better stage lighting, and fantastic worship teams.

Basically, in order for a church to survive, the article called for turning worship into entertainment excellent enough to rival whatever a person might be able to access at home with a flick of a button.

I would be tempted to agree with the writer of that article except for one thing—what I've seen among the Amish.

The Pew Forum on Religion and Public Life did a study of the retention rate of various world religions and denominations in 2008. A ranking, in descending order, of those retention rates showed Hindus at the top, with a retention rate of 84 percent. Jews and Muslims came next, tied at 76 percent. A sampling of other religions showed Catholics at 68 percent, Baptists at 60 percent, Pentecostals holding even at 50 percent, and Methodists losing ground at 46 percent. Atheists were at the bottom, with only a 30 percent retention rate within their belief system.

There was one religion that was not represented in the Pew Forum. The three most conservative Amish sects, which include the Old Order, Swartzentruber, and Andy Weaver Amish, had an average retention rate in 2010 of an astonishing 91 percent.

In other words, if the figures are accurate, the ultraconservative Amish, with their buggies, oil lamps, phone shanties, old-fashioned clothing, hard pews, no praise teams, no PowerPoint, and no evangelism, are thriving. They have a higher retention than any other known religion—and, in fact, the Amish population has been doubling every twenty years.

Why is this happening? How are they doing this? An easy answer is that they have large families who, on the whole, remain Amish. I am seeking the not-so-easy answer, the answer as to why this culture has such a high retention rate in the first place. Why do their kids stay? After all, the Amish are nothing like some world religions, in which leaving the faith can mean actually being put to death.

Being Amish is not forced on the children. They have a free choice to accept or reject the religion in which they were raised. The Amish are not at all evangelistic. It is not an easy life to accept. Half of the Englisch who do convert to Amish eventually leave. It's just too hard.

Strangely enough, from what I've privately heard and seen, Amish people don't even necessarily buy into all the rules of the Ordnung, or see a whole lot of sense in some of the restrictions that are placed upon them. As one Old Order Amish man told me privately, "I'm not really all that Amish in my heart."

This is not a blind faith, yet the people put up with major inconveniences and somehow manage to be growing rapidly.

The question is why.

The answer is different for every Amish youth who sells his or her car, accepts baptism, and pledges to obey God and the Ordnung for the rest of his or her life. Some stay because they love their families and don't want to disappoint them. Others stay because they truly believe it is the best way to heaven. Others choose this life because they want their own children to have the same advantages of being raised Amish that they did. Some stay for no other reason than that their spouse is Amish and does not wish to leave.

The amazing thing is that never before in the history of the Amish church have they had such a high retention rate. This seems to make no sense. With all the amazing technological and scientific advancements, why are so many Amish youths putting all this behind them?

I think part of it is that our society has become so unstable. After experiencing a taste of Englisch society during their running-around time, Amish young people want the protection and sanity of a slower culture. While spending time in a society that spurns boundaries and limitations of any sort, they begin to crave boundaries, and the Amish faith certainly has plenty of rules to safeguard people from themselves.

Ultimately, however, I think they are returning because it is so hard to leave a culture that cares for them so deeply—even if it means personal sacrifice.

Every church leadership I know wishes they had the magic formula for building a healthy church. Every preacher in every little church dotting our countryside wishes they could somehow find a way to turn the tide so that more people would start coming through the door.

I don't have the answers, but based on the retention rate and growth of the Amish church, apparently the answer does not rest in finding the best praise team or the best preacher. It doesn't even rest in having comfortable seats and air-conditioned churches. The Amish are led by untrained volunteers. The growth, then, certainly is not based on a well-educated staff and multiple ministry opportunities.

Amish church growth rests on a few ancient biblical principles that a lot of people never notice or choose to skim over:

Acts 2:41–42: "Those who accepted his message were baptized, and about three thousand were added to their number that day. They devoted themselves to the apostles' teaching and to fellowship, to the breaking of bread and to prayer."

This is a passage from the earliest days of Christianity. This is what was happening at a time when the church was growing like wildfire even in the face of persecution. 1) People were baptized, a ritual that visually represented the death, burial, and resurrection of Christ and also represented a giving up of self. This was also a ritual for which the Amish people were willing to be burned at the stake rather than renounce it. 2) They steadfastly followed the teachings of the apostles. 3) They spent time together in fellowship and sharing meals. 4) They worshipped together. 5) They prayed.

Based on the fact that the Amish, as a culture, are devoted to all five of these things, I think we have a hint as to why they are growing and why most of their children choose not to leave.

As one ex-Amish man told me, "Sometimes it's a little lonely out here in the world."

I once read an article about a retired couple from the United States who went to India to work as volunteers for Mother Teresa. Eventually they approached her with the idea of moving to India to stay and help her permanently. Her response surprised them. She told them to go back and work at home instead. Americans, she said, were some of the loneliest people in the world.

I often think about that statement when I'm sitting in Mary's kitchen with all her Amish neighbors and family coming and going. They are so wrapped up in one another's lives. Real lives. Real people. Americans might be some of the loneliest people in the world . . . but not those Americans known as the Amish.

Feeling like there are people who truly care about you, who

will be there for you if there are problems, who will support you if your family falls on hard times, and who will forgive you if you make a mistake . . . evidently those consolations are enough to overcome all the challenges and inconveniences of being Amish.

There is also the observation Henry made one day as we were discussing both Amish parenting and that the Amish are sometimes criticized for not being evangelistic.

"It has always seemed to me," the old man said, "that the best kind of evangelism is to simply live a life of integrity. From what I've seen over the years, that is also the most effective kind of parenting."

· VII ·

So, What's an
Englisch Parent to Do?

So, What's an
Englisch Parent to Do?

"I am quick to forgive my children because I often
need them to forgive me when I fail as a father."

—AMISH MINISTER

One of my concerns in writing this book was that I knew there
would be people wanting to chime in with stories about how
the Amish have this problem or that weakness. As I've said
several times, I know that the Amish are not a perfect people.
They are human and they are flawed, and they would be the
first to say so.

On the other hand, neither Paul nor I could see any value in
discussing the negatives. What we wanted to do was get to the
core of what actually *is* working in the Amish culture—especially
those things that are working *well*. That brings me back to the
word Ivan Miller used when we were talking at Keim Lumber
about the Amish work ethic and he said that Amish parents "intentionally" teach their children to work.

Intentional parenting. What does it mean? It means making intentional choices. Choosing what will and will not happen

in one's home. What will and will not be viewed in one's home. What will and will not be owned in one's home.

There are tons of parenting books out there with many different methods suggested for raising kids. I've read a lot of them, especially when I was raising my sons. Most of them left me feeling overwhelmed. A family counselor told me the other day that he felt the plethora of parenting books was the root cause behind "helicopter parenting" by those who overparent and try to be all things to their children all the time.

I think one reason I have grown fascinated with Amish parenting is because their kids tend to be such a joy to be around, and yet my Amish friends make it all look so easy. They seem so relaxed within their roles as parents.

The reason it looks easy is because Amish parenting isn't some step-by-step method to manipulate children into right behavior—it is simply a way of life that has proven to bring about good results over several centuries.

As I've interviewed my Amish friends, it is very clear to me that they aren't at all concerned about making their children happy, in an Englisch sense. The kind of happiness that is based on personal wants and expectations seems to be irrelevant to them.

Instead, they concentrate on helping their children grow into people of value—sons and daughters with integrity and compassion who know how to work and how to give. As I've said before—one of life's ironies is that children who grow up to be people of value tend to also be very happy people. On the other hand, children who have been placated, bribed, given no responsibility and too many possessions, who are not taught clear-cut values and rules or how to do a day's work . . . these children tend to become miserable fairly quickly.

Why do tourists come by the millions to Amish country? I agree with the Mennonite business owner. It isn't just for the pie. It is because our nation is starved to be around people of integrity who believe in unchanging principles.

I believe the children in our society are also starving—for meaning and integrity and loving structure in their lives. For too long we have fed our children the moral equivalent of cake and candy when they needed wholesome food with substance.

Children are also starving for the sense that they are a necessary part of a family who loves them. They are starving to feel that they have value and worth. They are starving for parents who'll talk with them for more than a few minutes per week and who will teach them how to live by example instead of leaving them to derive a world view from television and social media.

Do the Amish always live up to outsiders' expectations? Absolutely not. They don't even live up to their own expectations. Evidently, however, they have made some choices that matter to their children, because after a little "running around" time, those grown children are returning to their parents' faith and discipline in droves.

The importance of all these principles I've explored while researching Amish parenting was brought home to me just this week.

Twice a year, our congregation divides into home groups for a few weeks instead of meeting for Sunday-night service. It's a way to incorporate new people into our fellowship as well as get to better know people who already attend. As I was in the process of finishing this book, I was preparing to host a group in our home. This involved a small potluck dinner, general fellowship, and a period of Bible study. We had a houseful of people and nine of those were children from the age of twelve down to three. These children were from four different households.

I'd not had these particular children in my home before and was worried about how things would go during the adult Bible study time. I was expecting constant interruptions, a little tattling, and at least a few tears.

What I experienced instead were children who seemed pleased with the foods from the potluck we had and who happily played with the LEGOs, Lincoln Logs, and coloring books I provided. As the parents engaged in conversation and Bible study in another room, apart from a couple quick visits from the three-year-old for a reassuring hug and kiss from his parents, there were no tears, no tattling, no altercations, no whining. The children just . . . played.

By the time everyone was ready to leave, I noticed that the children had even worked together to put all the LEGOs and Lincoln Logs neatly away. Without being told.

The parents of three of these children do not have a television in their home. The other sets of parents put strict limits on their own and their children's access to television and other electronics. All do some gardening, are careful about limiting junk food, and try to eat as a family at least once a day. All three have strong relationships with grandparents and extended family and friends. Two of the mothers work part-time, but have figured out schedules with their husbands to put a parent in the home as much as possible.

These are families who are also givers. One mother is a nurse who loves her job, another is a social worker who is noted for her compassion. The mother who does not work outside her home is quick to help neighbors and friends—usually with all three of her children in tow as she does so. On our wall is a beautiful new wooden plaque that one of the fathers made us for Christmas, decorated with one of my husband's favorite scriptures. Another father is a physical therapist who has helped many of our congregation with their various aches and pains. These are families who reach out. They are giving people who also noticeably enjoy their children.

It is easy to be envious of the Amish and their interconnectedness, but this spring's home group emphasized to me that even in today's society, it does not take giving up electricity, cars, and technology and becoming Amish to have a supportive network of good people in one's life. What it does take is time and an intentional willingness to be available to others.

Raising children of value also does not happen by accident or by constantly gauging parental popularity. It takes getting control of one's life and family by making wise choices—sometimes very hard choices—instead of having our lives dictated by media or abdicating our responsibilities out of fatigue or fear.

Intentional parenting means having the courage to make choices that are *right* for our families instead of merely doing what is *easy*. Raising children who are not only happy but who are *more than happy* because they are growing into people of integrity and value does not happen by accident.

And yet . . .

Not every kid turns out well. Not even when they have earnest parents trying to do everything right. Not every kid raised poorly turns into a bad person. Individual choice is a powerful thing and yet many wonderful, dedicated parents are walking around with broken hearts, blaming themselves over decisions and choices their children have made.

Here is some comfort.

The story Jesus told about the prodigal son in Luke 15:11–31 is about a father who had done nothing wrong. He had worked hard, made a good living, loved his sons, and yet he ultimately had to watch his selfish youngest son walk away from all he had been taught. The boy spent every dime his father had given him on a lifestyle so sinful and wasteful that he was finally reduced to fighting over pig slop to survive.

Eventually the Bible says he came to his senses and went home intending to beg to be a servant on his father's farm, but instead of being angry and shouting recriminations at the boy for his foolish ways, the father welcomed him back with open arms. The Bible says that the father felt "compassion" for his son. He loved him and he forgave him.

The Amish nurture a culture of compassion and forgiveness, and have for more than five hundred years. This might well be the biggest reason so many Amish young people choose to eventually accept their parents' faith and all its restrictions in spite of all the interesting temptations available in our non-Amish society.

Of all the things I learned while researching this book, I think this might be the most important principle we can learn about parenting. Forgiveness is a two-way street in a family. Parents must often forgive their children, but sometimes it is the children who must forgive their parents. As that one Amish father explained, "I am quick to forgive my children because I often need them to forgive me when I fail as a father."

Mistakes are inevitable. Parenting is not an easy job. It is expensive, messy, time-consuming, and sometimes overwhelming. We parents make tens of thousands of decisions in the course of raising our children. No matter how hard we try, we are not going to get everything right.

Sometimes we have to forgive our children. Sometimes they have to forgive us. Sometimes we have to forgive our own parents. Sometimes they have to forgive us. Sometimes we have to forgive our spouses. Sometimes they have to forgive us.

And sometimes—no matter how consistent and conscientious we try to be—our kids make terrible decisions. They just do. When that happens, if we are to survive emotionally, we must forgive ourselves for our children's choices, pray for that prodigal child, and go on with our lives. After all, an awful lot of prodigals do eventually grow up and come to their senses. Remembering that can give a parent hope.

Gelassenheit. This is a word we frequently use in our house now, ever since my Amish friends taught it to me and it helps. *Gelassenheit.* We are not alone in this. God has a plan and He is in control.

Acknowledgments

I wish I could publicly thank the dozens of Amish friends who helped with this project, but for the sake of their requests for anonymity, I have carefully avoided revealing their identities. My Old Order Amish friend "Mary," who read and approved the final draft, thanked me for "hiding her behind the bush." I'm also grateful to my family for allowing me to include their personal stories.

My agent, Sandra Bishop, has carefully guided my career with knowledge, tenacity, and prayer. One of the things for which I am most grateful is that she had the wisdom to place me with editors who are not only publishing professionals but who also care passionately about the books they bring to their readers. It was Beth Adams, senior editor at Howard Books, who first saw the potential for a book about Amish parenting. Beth felt so strongly about this project that she helped work on it until a few days before she gave birth. Associate editor Amanda Demastus worked closely with Beth throughout and helped steer the book into the final stages of publication. These women guided me and gave me valuable input as I rewrote, reevaluated, and restructured these stories and principles, always checking for accuracy with Paul Stutzman—who generously shared his knowledge and great love for his people.

Our prayer is that this book will help parents raise children who are not just happy but who grow up to become "people of value."